b

D1458793

AUTHENTIC INDIAN DESIGNS

AUTHENTIC INDIAN DESIGNS

2500 ILLUSTRATIONS FROM REPORTS OF THE BUREAU OF AMERICAN ETHNOLOGY

EDITED BY

Maria Naylor

DOVER PUBLICATIONS, INC., NEW YORK

Published in Canada by General Publishing Company, Ltd., 30 Lesmill Road, Don Mills, Toronto, Ontario.
Published in the United Kingdom by Constable and Company, Ltd.

Authentic Indian Designs: 2500 Illustrations from Reports of the Bureau of American Ethnology, first published by Dover Publications, Inc., in 1975, is a new selection of illustrations from the first 44 *Annual Reports* of the Bureau. The original title pages of the first and 44th *Reports* read as follows:

First Annual Report of the Bureau of Ethnology to the Secretary of the Smithsonian Institute, 1879-'80, Government Printing Office, Washington, 1881.

Forty-fourth Annual Report of the Bureau of American Ethnology to the Secretary of the Smithsonian Institute, 1926-1927, United States Government Printing Office, Washington, 1928.

The picture selection and all the text in the present edition are by Maria Naylor.

DOVER *Pictorial Archive* SERIES

International Standard Book Number: 0-486-23170-4
Library of Congress Catalog Card Number: 74-17711

Manufactured in the United States of America
Dover Publications, Inc.
31 East 2nd Street
Mineola, N.Y. 11501

CONTENTS

INTRODUCTION

At the time of the discovery of the New World and the first encounters between Europeans and the Indian tribes of North America, the white man's curiosity about his world, its wonders and its inhabitants was both wide-ranging and intense. Reports from early explorers about the way of life of the inhabitants of the newly discovered lands generally included some descriptions of such arts and crafts as were then practiced by the people described, but while the Renaissance spirit of inquiry dictated that note be made of such manufactures, the same spirit worked against their being regarded as art. Although Albrecht Dürer said that the treasures from the court of Montezuma which he saw at Brussels in 1521 seemed more wondrous than the things spoken of in fairy tales, to the Hapsburg emperor and his creditors they were so much coinage-fodder. Until quite late in the Colonial period, explorers hoped to find great caches of treasure on the North American continent, treasures to rival those of Mexico and Peru; those who were slightly less visionary wanted land and furs. Throughout the Colonial period, destruction of those crafts extant when the white man came was part and parcel of the destruction of the Indian way of life as a whole. Native manufactures were quickly replaced by mass-produced trade goods, though some articles of Indian manufacture might be purchased from tribes that survived, if they were obviously utilitarian, like baskets, or superior to white products, like some kinds of tanned leather. Sometimes skills introduced by Europeans replaced native traditions, such as the floral embroidery patterns taught in French Canadian convents to Indian students, and later introduced into beadwork decoration. Any particular art, no matter how lengthy its tradition, could be lost quickly when the tribe decided to substitute trade goods for the native articles; or the make and decoration might be radically changed to capture a white market, and traditional methods again forgotten.

The beginning of interest in Indian art as art began at about the time that intelligent men in the more settled civilized portions of North America began to realize that it was quite possible that within a short span of years the Indians, their arts and their way of life altogether, might vanish. Among the few Americans or Europeans appalled at the thought were a number of artists or wealthy amateur sportsmen and scientists who made haste to visit the tribes that remained to any extent in a wild state. The most important of these was George Catlin, who brought back not only paintings, but actual artifacts and authentic Indians, with whom he formed an exhibition that traveled in the Eastern states and abroad. His published works, illustrated from his drawings, his portfolios of prints, and his collection of portraits (now in the Smithsonian) made the dress, weapons and decorations of the Plains tribes known to many, as did the published travels of Prince Maximilian of Weid-Neuweid, illustrated with fine aquatints after Karl Bodmer. The practice of collecting costumes, weapons, robes and other articles of Indian manufacture for studio props and detail study continued among later generations of artists who painted the West, down to Frederic Remington and the artists of the twentieth century, many of whom valued their collections highly for aesthetic as well as scientific reasons. About the middle of the nineteenth century a great deal of attention began to be focused on the various burial and temple mounds of the Ohio and Mississippi, especially after it became clear to those scholars who were not hopelessly ensnared by theories of colonizing Phoenicians, wandering tribes of Israelites and other less likely groups, that these impressive structures and their often surprisingly rich contents should be attributed to the direct ancestors of tribes in the area. The earliest reports of the Bureau of Ethnology contained a number of learned papers on the Mound Builders and their remains, all firmly declaring the mounds to be of Indian origin. The writings of Henry Schoolcraft inspired the Indian epic *Hiawatha* by Longfellow, and the ten years of intensive warfare among the Plains tribes, especially the western Sioux, following the Civil War drew the attention of much of Europe as well as the eastern States to the embattled tribes. The Bureau of Ethnology was founded in 1879, just three years after the Battle of the Little Bighorn. It began its task of collecting artifacts, recording traditions and making a scholarly study of a way of life just on the point of vanishing. Of the many monographs and papers published throughout the more than forty years that the Bureau issued an annual report, many are still considered classics or even "the bible" of their field. There is possibly no way of estimating how much of our knowledge and understanding of the artistic traditions of American Indian life, to say nothing of the preservation of countless works of art, we owe to the work of the Bureau and the scholars who worked for it or contributed to its publications. It is from their papers in the Bureau *Reports* that all the illustrations in the present book have been selected.

The arrangement of the book is very simple: the first section is devoted to the largely prehistoric art of the eastern United States, concentrating on the arts of the cultures that arose in the great river networks of the Mississippi and Ohio Valleys. Thereafter the sections are arranged geographically: The Eastern Woodlands, centering on the Great Lakes area; the Plains; The Pacific Northwest, Eskimo art of both Alaska and the Canadian interior, and British Columbia; and lastly the Southwest, both ancient and modern. The works illustrated were made of many materials, from woven wools and beaded buckskin to basketry, pottery and carved stone. Of particular interest are numerous forms of masks from two areas,

the Northwest Coast and the Southwest. In many cases, the objects illustrated were collected from the original owners or even makers, and the designs thus are not only of irreproachable authenticity, but in many cases antedate the period of white influence. At any rate, they were not made for "souvenirs" or trade, but for actual use. Most of the objects shown on the following pages were in the final analysis utilitarian—they were weapons, or utensils or clothing, or were intended to be employed in some ceremonial or ritual, or to serve some totemic purpose. Few tribes produced anything specifically and separately as a work of art or for purely aesthetic reasons. (One exception might be various Eskimo carvings, made apparently for pleasure, though not for creating "art.") On the other hand, the love of color and ornamentation ran throughout Indian life, and wherever and whenever the material level of culture or the amount of leisure time permitted, objects made for use were decorated. Any tribe that produced some particularly finely made or decorated ware had a ready trade with less proficient neighbors. Perhaps it was the ultimately utilitarian purpose of many crafts that led to the loss of some arts, such as pottery and basketry, among tribes who began to acquire metal trade pots from the whites. The new utensils served the purpose as well, and left the craftsmen free of all the labor that went into not only the manufacture of the objects, but the gathering and preparation of raw materials as well. The aesthetic interest, always secondary, would be shifted elsewhere, not simply lost or allowed to die.

There has been a definite tendency to draw a sharp line between the work of tribes before continuous or prolonged contact with white culture, and that following it; only the former, or at any rate, only work made exclusively in the earlier tradition, is accepted as genuinely Indian. A work that shows European influences or employs trade materials to a great extent is classed as decadent. The quality of much Indian work declined after contact with white civilization because their whole life, their whole social and economic system, was being disrupted, not because innovations or new materials were in themselves harmful to Indian design. The Indians had been accustomed to borrowing designs and techniques from one another, and often changes in a style of decoration just as drastic and complete as any caused by the impact of the white man's goods can be detected in earlier cultures, as in the Southwest or among the Mound Builders. In particular, the Indians loved bright colors and startling contrast. Most scholars of Indian arts writing for the Bureau of Ethnology or contemporary with it unanimously deplore the use of aniline dyes in weaving, basketry and pottery, which was introduced about the close of the nineteenth century. Similar cries of anguish, it should be noted, were made about the use of aniline colors in needlework by late-Victorian ladies.

Finally, many of the designs given in this volume have a symbolic meaning, and where this could be determined with any degree of sureness, it has been given; many meanings had been lost or distorted, however, by the time the Bureau was making its studies. At times, Indians of the same tribe could not agree over the meaning of various symbols; the same design might have many interpretations, and one idea might be represented by a number of symbols. Color itself was frequently symbolic, but the symbolism varied, quite naturally, from tribe to tribe.

Many symbols were related to personal "medicine," and were often closely guarded secrets; since these often referred to individual happenings, such as dreams or visions, the interpretation of the "owner" of the design was sometimes necessary to comprehend its meaning.

All the identifications and explanations of objects in this book are based on the text of the original reports. Spellings of Indian terms have been regularized, with diacritical marks omitted. The names of tribes appear as they are given in *The Indian Tribes of North America* by John R. Swanton (Bureau of American Ethnology *Bulletin 145*, 1952).

PREHISTORIC ART OF THE EASTERN WOODLANDS

Man came from the Old World to the New via the land bridge that stretched from Siberia to Alaska during the periods when glaciation reached its greatest extent. Not only did the immense glaciers lower the level of the seas between Asia and North America so that the land connection was exposed, but the actual path palaeolithic man most probably used escaped being covered by ice (perhaps because of low precipitation, since much of the surrounding ocean was already locked up in glaciers). These palaeo-Indians were not pioneers consciously seeking a new land, but hunters following herds of large game animals who crossed by the same path they used. When did they arrive? Perhaps forty thousand years ago; certainly more than twelve to thirteen thousand. Within these two limits lies ground for controversy.

The possessions they brought with them were slight: knowledge of how to hunt or trap large animals by cooperative efforts, by a stampede or surround, as well as with spears; a comparatively crude stone-age technology; knowledge of how to survive in arctic or subarctic conditions, a social organization suited to a nomadic life, and doubtless a few vague ideas and speculations about the universe and the supernatural. When the big game animals died out, the palaeo-Indians adapted themselves to new conditions, and developed various culture patterns suited to particular climates and geographical regions: in general, one for the desert regions of the western half of the continent, another for the wooded areas east of the Mississippi.

This new period is called by archaeologists the *Archaic*, and it is entirely postglacial. Life was based on hunting, fishing, shellfish gathering and plant collecting. This period is represented by a myriad of sites scattered throughout the eastern half of North America. Although local variations existed, depending upon what sources of food were available in the immediate neighborhood, there was a uniformity of principle behind the food-gathering techniques of all these peoples of the Archaic culture: an intensive harvesting of whatever foods happened to be seasonally in surplus or abundance, without overexploiting any one animal or vegetable source. About 1000 B.C. the *Woodland Period* began in the area of the Ohio and upper Mississippi Valleys, fanning out to reach as far north as Illinois and as far east as West Virginia, replacing or modifying the Archaic tradition. The Woodland tradition produced two dominant culture patterns, the earlier one named the Adena, and the later the Hopewell; the two evidently coexisted for a period, but the Hopewell lasted longer, until perhaps 750 A.D. The people of the Adena culture apparently did not practice agriculture, but their food-gathering methods were so efficient that they were able to develop a settled and large population, with several classes of society, including such specialized groups as priests and artisans. The Adena culture centered upon an area located in present-day southern Ohio, northern Kentucky and northwestern West Virginia. The nucleus of the Hopewell culture was situated in southern Ohio and Illinois, but Hopewell influences were felt as far away from this center as Minnesota, New York, Florida and Louisiana. The Hopewell culture, which did practice agriculture, intensified and elaborated the traits recognizable among the Adena peoples. They carried on a widespread trade in exotic materials, and made mortuary offerings of often astounding richness. The peoples of the Woodland tradition belong to that vague group of peoples designated as Mound Builders, as do the peoples of the tradition which succeeded them, the Mississippian, which began about 500 A.D. The mounds of the Woodland tradition were primarily for burials, although enormous earthworks were also built; through successive burials the mounds often reached a height of 70 feet. On the other hand, the mounds of the Mississippian culture were as a rule built surrounding a central plaza, and supported temples or palaces—a sort of civic center. The Mississippian developed in part from both the Archaic and Woodland heritages, but showed

a number of significant innovations; intensification of maize agriculture and large permanent towns and villages, in addition to the platform mounds surrounding central spaces. The centers of the new culture were in the lower Mississippi Valley, but its influences are found all over much of the Eastern Woodlands area. Meso-American links and influences are evident in this culture, particularly in new pottery vessel forms and decorative techniques, but it is not quite evident by what route or by what means these influences arrived. Most probably it was not by a continuous geographic link, such as a trail through Texas and Louisiana. This Temple Mound period lasted from about 700 to about 1700; in some areas, patches of the culture survived into the period of European invasion and occupation. For the first time it is possible to connect the Indians of a prehistoric period with those of more recent times, since it has been determined that nearly all these Temple Mound people can most probably be grouped, into the five historic language families Algonkian, Siouan, Iroquoian, Caddoan and Muskogean.

Much of our knowledge of the art of these early cultures is based on burial offerings placed in the mounds with the dead, and is of necessity of such material as can survive several centuries, or even millennia, of inhumation in various kinds of soil conditions; in a word, it is mostly ceramic. (Much pottery from the Gulf Coast and Florida has also been recovered from shell middens, but the same conditions apply.) Pottery and pottery remains are so much the archaeologists' staple that they furnish material for countless jokes as well as dating procedures. Nevertheless they are especially useful in locating vanished people and in defining their geographical limitations and migration patterns. Pottery is too fragile to travel well, so fragments remain in plenty on every occupation site, while the broken pieces themselves are virtually indestructible. While vessels are often abandoned because they are unsuitable for transport, new ones in exactly the same style will be made at the new home wherever proper raw materials are available. There are, of course, several disadvantages in relying too heavily upon pottery as evidence, especially when dealing with peoples like those of the Woodland and Mississippian traditions, about whom nothing is known from other sources. Parallelism can occur in pottery of peoples widely separated in time and space, but of a like grade of culture, provided they have access to similar types of clay. Interchanges by trade (although most pottery of this period was not suitable as trade items, for reasons given above), multiple occupation of sites at different periods by different peoples, adoption of pottery-making captives or refugees (doubtless a frequent occurrence, since women, the prime targets for capture, were also the pottery makers), the amalgamation of communities—all these factors can create difficulties in interpretation, especially where there are no independent means for checking attributions and correcting judgments. The same geographical area can be occupied simultaneously or successively by two groups of peoples. Then, too, while separate groups of people have produced nearly identical wares, portions of the same people have produced widely different types and grades of pottery.

The pottery of the Eastern Woodlands was separated into groups mainly geographical in nature by the scholars of the Bureau of Ethnology, largely because establishing a chronology was extremely difficult for them, while the point of origin was comparatively easy to check. The excavations of most of the mounds in the nineteenth century can best be described as looting or plundering, even when undertaken for the best of motives and in the spirit of scientific inquiry. Many of the items described in the studies by the Bureau of Ethnology had come from private collections, and only the place of excavation could be given with any amount of accuracy. One prime difficulty is that certain of the areas, such as Kentucky, Tennessee and other portions of the "Southern Appalachian group," plus the lower Mississippi area and the Gulf Coast, might show influences of both Woodland and Mississippian traditions experienced at different periods.

Since all arts are not symmetrical and equally developed—different peoples choosing to concentrate on different arts and crafts and to neglect others—inferior wares from one locality do not necessarily mean that the culture was in its entirety inferior; for example, the rich Adena and Hopewell cultures of the Ohio Valley had rather poor pottery. As a general rule, the pottery of the North is cruder than that of the South, though Gulf Coast pottery is frequently quite crude, and occasional specimens from the North can be quite fine. This can be partially ascribed to the fact that the food supply in the South, because of climate and more intensive agriculture, was more stable and easily gathered, and the population settled, factors which enabled them to devote more time to pottery. (Again, chronology must be figured in: the Mississippian tradition, to which most of the pottery described as southern belongs, came later than the cultures of the Ohio Valley, and also enjoyed possible influences from Meso-America. Also, the Ohio Valley people concentrated on other arts, such as stone carving.) Certainly it is true that with the exception of the ceramics produced in the ancient Southwest. (discussed in a later section) the pottery of the Mississippian tradition, or the Middle Mississippi Valley Group as it was called earlier, was the finest produced in pre-Columbian North America. The pottery-making tradition in this area lasted from its origins about 1000 B.C. until after the European discovery of America, but the introduction of metal pots among the whites' trade goods soon put an end to the craft.

The area classifications used by the Bureau of Ethnology to describe this pottery included the Middle Mississippi Valley Group, Lower Mississippi Valley Group, Ohio Valley Group, Gulf Coast Group, Southern Appalachian, Atlantic-Algonquian and Iroquoian. So far as use goes, the vessels were divided into a number of categories: domestic (cooking and storage utensils, sugar and salt-making vessels), industrial (tools and implements), sacerdotal (for funeral rites and burial offerings), ornamental (beads, pendants, ear and lip plugs), trivial or diversional (toys, figurines, gaming articles). Somewhat difficult to classify according to this list are certain Middle Mississippi Valley Group wares: some vases of refined and unusual shape (probably made for private but not ordinary domestic use), as well as effigy vases in the form of kneeling hunchbacks and heads of men, beasts and grotesque beings (which may be either sacerdotal, diversional or possibly domestic wares in unusual shapes). Although many vessels are highly ornamental and elaborately decorated, it is not thought likely that any vessel was manufactured for purely ornamental purposes. (This does not refer, of course, to beads, pendants and so forth, which were ornaments, although they may have had talismanic significance as well.)

The most important of the classes of ceramics, whether considered by the regional or chronological division, was that of the Middle Mississippi Valley Group, which despite the all-embracing name was actually made by many tribes and linguistic groups whose descendants were probably to be found among the tribes still occupying the region when the white man came. The present-day states covered in this region include parts of Arkansas, Mississippi, Illinois, Kentucky and Tennessee. Closely related items are found along the Gulf Coast and Tampa Bay, and wares bearing decided influences of the culture are found as far north as Chicago, east to Pittsburgh, and south and west into Louisiana and Texas. Discoveries have also been made in Missouri, Iowa, Indiana and Alabama. The characteristics of the pottery are naturally best defined at the center of the area, but the distribution of the ideas embodied was facilitated by the great open river waterways, though whether by diffusion or by trade is still disputed.

The ware itself was elegant and varied in shape. Decoration took a variety of forms: fanciful modification of form (human or animal shapes), relief ornament, intaglio figures, surface decoration principally in color—a real innovation in the ceramic art of this part of North America. It was applied either by paint or by colored slips, and was mostly in white, red, brown and black. Other distinctive traits were a particular form of long-necked carafe, and a strong leaning toward the grotesque, both in form and in decoration. In evidence of this taste are bowls made in the shape of birds, fish, reptiles and shells; some of these forms must apply to various mythologic conceptions, symbolisms or superstitions. In the same vein may perhaps be included the effigy vases of men and figures of monsters, including vases evidently representing the heads of the dead.

The Southern Appalachian Group was the name the Bureau of Ethnology applied to finds in Georgia, South Carolina, North Carolina, Alabama, Florida and Tennessee. One especially characteristic form from this region was stamped ware, with decoration applied at random or all over by means of carved paddles. This type of decoration was perpetuated into modern times by the Catawbas, Cherokees, Choctaws, Chickasaws and Seminoles. Other marks of Southern Appalachian Group ware included novel shapes; a rather peculiar style of decoration, intermingling local and exotic forms; the rare use of shells and stones for inlaying; and the making of figurines somewhat reminiscent of figures from Mexico. A characteristic form of vessel was a large cauldron or cook pot; such pots were often used as coffins for burying the dead.

Iroquoian and Algonquian refer to groups of tribes classified by language. The Iroquois in particular were extremely widespread, and their seat of power extended from Hudson's Bay almost to the Gulf, with the center of population in New York State. The cultural remains of this group are strongly individual and well marked, with pottery the most important feature. In general, Iroquoian products fall in with the simple ware of the northeastern area, but they present certain striking and distinctive characteristics of shape and decoration. Within the group, many local variations in form, ornament and composition have been distinguished. The wares were often decorated with textured paddle stamps or with a cord-wrapped wheel. Other forms of decoration were simple and limited, employing mostly archaic rectilinear designs, often incised; curved lines seldom occur.

The culture identified as Ohio Valley Group falls into the Woodland tradition (about 1000 B.C. to about 750 A.D.). The pottery is rather poorly made, but is associated with other finds that indicate a rich culture and far-flung trade. The pottery has been classified as generally simple and inartistic, but some unique terracotta figurines discovered in mounds in this area have proved a fascinating exception to this rule.

The Gulf Coast Group refers to the inhabitants of an area around the Gulf of Mexico from the Mississippi Delta east to the Pensacola Bay area of Florida. Often several varieties of vessels, obviously the products not only of different tribes, but of different linguistic groups, are found on the same site, complicating study of the area. However, of the pottery finds as a whole it can be said that a great variety of forms of vessels were made, though inferior in number and scope to the shapes of the Middle Mississippi Valley Group, and few traces of painted vessels have turned up. Animals or animal features modeled in the round were often attached to vases, and are frequently found associated with incised designs on pots, which, though highly conventionalized, appear to represent the same animals. Features such as decoration with stamps were evidently introduced from the Southern Appalachian Group. A form of decoration in which the designs were punched into the fabric of the pot by a series of dots was also practiced in parts of this area.

The Lower Mississippi Valley Group was allied to both the Middle Mississippi Valley Group and the Gulf Coast Group, with possible Mexican and even Pueblo influences. Its most distinctive product was pottery of a black color with designs incised with almost mechanical precision.

Other artistic remains from the mounds have also been necessarily for the most part of materials which could survive long periods of burial in the earth. Some of the most spectacular of these are stone carvings from the Ohio Valley area, from the period of the Hopewell culture. The considerable degree of technical skill shown in these carvings, coupled with an advanced aesthetic feeling, led early theorists to suppose that they were made by peoples of a different stock from those Indians found still occupying the area in historic times. Other tests proved the continuity of lineage from prehistoric to recent inhabitants, while some scholars even denied any artistic inferiority among the latter-day Indians when compared with their mound-building ancestors. Most of the carvings are pipe bowls, often in stone brought from a great distance, an evidence of widespread trade at that early date. They represent many

natural objects—birds, animals, human figures, grotesque beings. In the nineteenth century many of these birds and animals were misidentified as exotic species, often tropical, opening the way for the concoction of farfetched theories of migrations from the Caribbean or Central America, or trade with that area. More sober examinations have given these pieces the names of entirely local species. In many cases, the carvings are probably not meant to be of any particular species at all; the artist may have had no specific bird in mind, and many of the animals were probably totemic rather than decorative in origin. There is also no reason for believing that human features are not equally conventionalized in most cases, although occasional examples of individualized portrait heads do seem to occur. In any event, extreme realism was quite probably not an aim of the creators, and failure to achieve an absolutely naturalistic representation should by no means be considered a failure of skill.

Still other art objects which have survived from mound burials were, paradoxically enough, made in a quite fragile, perishable material. These are shell carvings, in particular pendants, gorgets or breastplates which are found in mounds of the Temple Mound period going back to about 1400 A.D. By the seashore, or by the banks of great rivers where shells of great size are plentiful, they were thought of only as utensils or as material for making tools. Carried far inland in trade, these shells became objects of great value, and were used to make precious ornaments. (Seashells have been found as far inland as the Rocky Mountains.) Both freshwater and saltwater shells were used to manufacture beads and decorations. Other objects made were vessels, spoons, knives, fish hooks, tweezers and pins. Many types of ornaments have survived: gorgets; nose, ear and wrist ornaments; and ornaments that apparently were part of head-dresses. The different forms are difficult to date, and the geographical distribution spreads from Texas to Canada. Some are definitely pre-Columbian, while others show signs of European influences, or have been found in burials with objects of European manufacture. Among the great number of designs found engraved on pendants or gorgets, a handful recur with consistent frequency. These include: the cross, which probably has reference to directions, or perhaps to a tree; the scalloped disk, which may represent the sun; the bird, an important symbol with all peoples, although the specific birds shown are difficult to identify, and may be totemic in origin; the spider, which figures in many Indian legends; and the serpent, which had a fascination for primitive man, and played an important part in Indian myths and religion. It was important to the people of the mounds even in periods predating the engraved shells, for a number of mounds were constructed in the shape of a coiled serpent. A few representations of the human face and figure appear on engraved shells, both highly stylized and showing definite Meso-American influence.

THE EASTERN WOODLANDS

The Indians who inhabited the Eastern Woodlands when the first Europeans arrived bore the brunt of the earliest and all the successive waves of arrivals, settlements and migrations. Consequently most of their handiwork, being of material more perishable than pottery, has vanished. Where scattered remnants of tribes survived, they often continued to practice traditional crafts, often using trade goods obtained from the whites, following traditional designs much influenced by European styles or simply copied from them with an eye to trading or selling these articles.

Because they had associations with political agreements, and a monetary value as well, some objects made of wampum by these eastern tribes survived. Originally, the beads were made by hand from certain shells, usually in white and black (actually purple), and occasionally red as well. Each color had a definite relative value to beads of other colors, but the absolute values fluctuated. The making of wampum is recorded in the earliest European writings on Indian customs; doubtless, it was its use as currency rather than as decoration that attracted so much notice. Both uses were widespread on the North American continent at the time of the first white arrival. Europeans soon adopted the shells as currency in their trade with the Indians, and were more than willing to take it in exchange for all manner of trade goods, for they could in turn purchase furs with it. In fact, they soon set to manufacturing it by more efficient mechanical means. Today, few of the surviving articles of wampum appear to predate this introduction of mechanical turning of the beads on a lathe.

With the Indians, use of wampum for currency and trade was simultaneous and indeed interchangeable: witness King Philip's famous wampum coat that served him as a wearable treasury. When he needed money, he cut pieces or strings of wampum off the bottom. Wampum belts were also used to keep records and to register treaties, councils and agreements; in fact, no treaty or agreement was regarded as valid unless wampum in varying amounts changed hands. Some of these belts that record specific events are mnemonic, others purely symbolic. During speeches at councils, sentences or phrases were accented by the distribution of strings of wampum. Only the most important part of a speech would be marked by the gift of a belt of wampum. Various of these belts contain enormous numbers of beads, running into the thousands, even when they are obviously no longer complete. Some wampum belts remained in the possession of the tribes that had made them, or had received them at councils until the end of the nineteenth century. Each year a few beads were destroyed as sacrifices at annual rites. When the colonists began to mint coins and print paper money, they ceased to manufacture wampum beads for trade; by that time it had become a lost art to the Indians as well. As a consequence, few of the belts still in existence are complete.

Shells of various types were the original material from which various tribes living around the Great Lakes manufactured the beads with which they decorated their clothing, moccasins and various pieces of equipment, but the traditional, laboriously worked shell beads were quickly abandoned for the use of trade beads. Various of these tribes, such as the Ojibwa, Chippewa, Winnebago and Menominee, were noted for their beadwork even until the end of the nineteenth century. The designs used were based on both traditional geometric patterns and on curvilinear floral and other life-form designs derived from European embroidery patterns taught in French-Canadian convents. Much of the most elaborate beadwork was intended for, or was especially worn during, various religious ceremonies and dances. Contrary to the usages of many other tribes, whose dancers wore as little as possible during ceremonials, the Ojibwa and Menominee in particular were elaborately garbed for dances, and looked upon disregard of dress as sacrilegious. Once strict regulations existed within the tribes regarding the wearing of adornments and clothing; later all rules became confused, and the following of personal fancy was allowed free play. Clothing, moccasins, garters, necklaces and armbands were often profusely beaded, or woven entirely of beads, and bags entirely covered with beads were once common. Garters were essentially part of a dancer's costume, and a wealthy Indian might wear as many as a dozen beaded bags at once to a dance. Since bead-

working by hand was very tedious, these sumptuously beaded bags were a very obvious display of personal wealth. Beaded designs on clothes were usually simpler, and were stitched directly on the cloth or skin of the garment.

Woven beadwork was made without the aid of a pattern, the worker relying on her eye and memory to make the design come out right and have new motifs start in the right place. The usual designs found on garters were diamond and lozenge shapes, frets, vines and meanders. Frequently traditional geometric and realistic designs introduced from European sources were combined in one piece. These tribes had a traditional color symbolism for their beadwork, knowledge of which was handed down to recent times, but on occasion other colors were substituted when the usual ones were not available in trade beads; apparently this did not impair the meaning of the design.

A few examples of essentially minor arts are also included, such as birchbark transparencies, sometimes used as beading patterns, and silk ribbon appliqué work employing trade cloth and ribbons.

Two drawings are included illustrating Iroquois myths about Atotarho, an actual Indian contemporary with the historical Hiawatha (sixteenth century). His qualities, however, were strongly contrasted to those of Longfellow's epic hero. This fund of folklore and myths was at the close of the nineteenth century the principal monument remaining of the once mighty Iroquois.

THE PLAINS AREA

The Plains area of North America has been occupied by people dependent upon hunting since the palaeo-Indians crossed the land bridge between Siberia and Alaska on the track of big game. Their essentially nomadic way of life has left little in the way of tangible traces. What is thought of today as the "traditional" way of life of the Plains Indian —the bands of mounted warriors, dashing in their warpaint, clad in splendidly decorated and fringed costumes with plumed warbonnets, the tribes constantly on the move during three fourths of the

year after the migrating buffalo herds, the skillful and daring buffalo hunters—was actually a fairly late development, and depended ultimately upon the horse, obtained from the Spanish settlements in the Southwest. Once possession of the horse made the hunting of the buffalo increasingly efficient, many of the Plains tribes came to be dependent upon this animal for virtually all their needs: clothing, food, shelter, tools and weapons. This buffalo-based economy was soon seriously disrupted by the introduction of trade goods, such as guns, liquor and manufactured items. Because of the relatively high value of even the most tawdry trade items against buffalo robes or furs, the Indians were required to slaughter far more animals, far more wastefully, than had been necessary when they hunted only for food and raw materials.

Apparently some of the tribes that the white settlers found occupying the Plains area had "always" been there; such were the Blackfeet and various allied tribes. Others had recently taken to the Plains and the life of nomadic hunters, abandoning their semisedentary, semiagricultural villages upon the acquisition of sufficient numbers of horses to mount their hunters and warriors; or had been driven out into the area by tribes yet farther east, themselves under pressure from European settlement, or from other tribes who had become possessed of guns and ammunition. These tribes were extremely diverse in language and dialects, but communication was possible throughout the area by means of sign language, the lingua franca of the Plains. In the late nineteenth century, many ethnologists and scientists studied the sign language of the Plains with great interest, noting in particular the similarities between many of the signs and the pictographs used to express like ideas and phrases. Many of the designs in this section of the book are taken from various kinds of pictographs made by Plains Indians. The famous "winter counts," buffalo robes which recorded the history of a particular tribe or band, used this form of picture writing, though many of the pictographs are more mnemonic than representational—it was necessary to know and memorize the facts behind the drawing before it could be interpreted correctly. Also included are some drawings of winter counts made by individuals,

and some drawings from an Indian autobiography. These are somewhat more pictorial and representational in character, although specific knowledge of the events depicted is necessary for strictly accurate interpretation. The same is true of some Indian drawings of incidents at the battle of the Little Bighorn. Of all pictographs, those most closely related to the sign language are the various rosters of Sioux bands. The symbols that accompany the heads of many of the warriors would have been indicated by similar hand signals in sign language when the warrior announced his name to tribesmen of a different language group. Designs painted on tipi (teepee) covers might be pictographic-historic, such as that on half of the famous Kiowa Battle Tipi, or they might be symbolic in character. The symbolism might identify the owner of the tipi to those who read the decorations, or it might refer to some personal "medicine" of the owner. Often the decorations were dictated by visions.

Some decorated shirts typical of Plains Indian clothing are shown, though each has decorations that make it in some way special. One is an example of the "ghost shirt," worn in the Ghost Dance uprising of 1890 in the belief that the "medicine" of the decorations would render the wearer invulnerable to white bullets. Another type of shirt shown in several examples is the Apache medicine shirt; this has a slit in the middle for the head to go through, as in a poncho. Although in painting the decorations on these shirts, the maker made use of many typical and traditional symbols, the decoration of each was unique and determined by the wearer. Once the Apache "shaman" put on one of these shirts, he ceased to be a man and became a power.

THE NORTHWEST COAST, ALASKA AND THE ARCTIC REGIONS

Geography is the one unifying bond between the peoples in this section, for it is difficult to imagine greater contrasts than that between the rigorous life of the Eskimos and tribes inhabiting arctic re-

gions, and the wealth accumulated by some of the tribes along the Pacific Coast, where a continuous round of "conspicuous consumption" once accounted for elements of both mobility and stability in society. Eskimo and Northwest coastal tribes alike have made significant aesthetic contributions, the latter principally in weaving and objects of carved wood, the former in carvings in various materials such as bone, tusks and teeth of various aquatic mammals (notably walrus ivory). In this region as well, in present-day British Columbia, was found one of the principal areas of basket making and design in North America, practiced by various tribes of the Interior Salish.

NORTHWEST COAST CARVING AND PAINTING (pp. 71–79)

Works by members of the three northernmost tribes of the Northwest Coast group are given here: the Haida, Tlingit and Tsimshian. The economy of these tribes was based on gathering and fishing (both for river salmon and deep-sea fish). The abundance of food available from these sources permitted a rich material culture ordinarily to be found only among peoples who practiced some kind of food cultivation. Indeed, on occasion these people stockpiled so much wealth that it became a status symbol to give away or destroy as much property as possible; the most thorough and spectacular manner of doing this was at the ceremonial gift distribution called the "potlatch." Household utensils, canoes and practically all objects utilized by these tribes were elaborately decorated; this is especially true of wooden objects. Only animal motifs were used. Each design generally consisted of a combination of various parts of an animal's body in forms easily recognized, though highly conventionalized. The artist represented what appeared to him to be the essential parts of the animal with little regard for their actual arrangement in space. In general, the purpose of this dissection and distortion was to fit the whole animal as nearly as possible into the decorative field to be covered. One characteristic of the art of this region is the filling of virtually every square millimeter of space with some portion of the design.

The Northwest Coast was one of the areas of North America where the manufacture and use of masks was of particular importance, both in cultural and artistic terms. Masks from this area rank among the handsomest produced by any culture anywhere. Some of the basic motivations behind the production of masks by mankind in general can be applied not just to the masks of this area, but to those of other American Indian tribes as well. The ultimate idea of a mask is that of a shield or protection for the face, and decoration of any kind was at first secondary to the idea of protection or disguise. Eventually, along with the purpose of inspiring terror in those who viewed the wearer of the mask, both mask and wearer gained a moral power. These masks were used in many ways: in warfare, to terrify the enemy, to display personal emblems, as totems or heraldic symbols; in religious rituals and shamanic rites; in secret societies; at festivals for the personation of supernatural beings; for buffoonery and comic relief.

The ornamentation of these masks employed a wide range of conventionalized figures. Masks played a very important part in shamanic paraphernalia, especially among the Tlingit, where shamans wielded tremendous power (far more so than among the Haida or Tsimshian) and each shaman had several masks. Also used were dancing masks and headdresses, helmets for warfare and decoys for hunting. Among the Haida, for instance, masks were found in considerable number in all villages, and the Haida carved masks for the use of other tribes in the area as well.

Because of the power of individual shamans and of the class as a whole, shamanic masks were of particular importance. They were used in essentially all the functions of these shamans: curing the sick, locating supplies of food, obtaining help from spirits against enemies in war, and so forth. Often shamans in hostile towns dressed up in complete paraphernalia and fought each other by spirits. These masks often had, in addition to the principal figure, one or more smaller ones which represented subsidiary spirits, supposed to strengthen special features or faculties of the shaman who wore them—a figure around the eyes strengthened sight; around the nose, smell; and so on. These were usually figures of some small animals; one highly regarded by the Indians was the wood worm, admired for its ability to bore through solid planks.

THE ESKIMO OF ALASKA AND THE HUDSON'S BAY REGION (pp. 80–102)

Though the migrations to the New World from the Old via the land bridge between Siberia and Alaska may have begun as long as 40,000 years ago, studies conducted by ethnologists and anthropologists have demonstrated that the Eskimo who live today in the area where the migrations were made are relatively recent arrivals. Anthropological evidence testifies to the fact that the forebears of various Eskimo tribes left Siberia only after the development of certain specific physical traits in response to Arctic conditions, such as the epicanthic fold across the lower part of the eye.

The Eskimo, more than almost any other people, have had their lives conditioned by the area and climate they live in. Formerly every aspect of their lives was carefully fitted into their physical world and the demands made upon them by nature. Within the past century or so, the lives of the Alaskan Eskimo have been greatly changed by contact with numerous sailors, hunters and traders. Even the Hudson's Bay Eskimo, in their comparative isolation, experienced many changes as a result of their contacts with traders and missionaries. By the late nineteenth century, one was forced to go far to the north around the shores of Hudson's Bay to find pure-blooded Eskimo. Their language was also affected, for the traders and missionaries insisted that the Eskimo accept white pronunciation of many words to simplify their difficult language for the intruders.

At the time when the collections of artifacts and the observations on Alaskan Eskimo life and culture were being made in the seventies and eighties of the last century, many of the traditions and underlying symbolism connected with the objects had already been forgotten. Nonetheless, the more than ten thousand ethnologic items gathered have proved of immense value to anthropologists and students. The adaptation of the Eskimo to his land and climate required a great variety of tools developed for specific functions: hunting and fishing, the making of weapons, the sewing of garments in particular. Though they were utilitarian, the manufacture of these tools also offered an opportunity for art. The enforced leisure of long arctic winters offered an occasion for the making and decorating of tools and artifacts. Alaskan Eskimos were admired for their remarkable dexterity in working wood, bone, ivory and reindeer horn; implements for hunting and household purposes, made for the most part with the simplest and crudest of tools, were handsome and elaborately ornamented. Where ivory was plentiful, it was also used for items of no utilitarian purpose: toys, games or carvings made for pleasure alone. This artistic ability was especially evident in the people living between the Yukon Delta and the lower Kuskokwim Valley.

Much artistic expression went into clothing, another item ultimately utilitarian, but which offered much scope for decoration and decorative effects. Even the Eskimo of Hudson's Bay, living in a much more rugged country, without the supplies of marine ivory available to Alaskan tribes, set much store by handsomely decorated garments, such as a fur frock with an edging of pear-shaped pieces of ivory on the skirt. Tribes of Indians living in the area of Hudson's Bay also made gaily decorated skin clothing, though their tailoring abilities did not approach that of the Eskimo.

Masks were another artistic production of the Alaskan Eskimo. These were made in all sizes for the celebration of the many feasts that were such an important feature of their social life, and that served to enliven the cold darkness of arctic winter evenings. Some masks no more than a few inches high were intended to be worn on the fingers of women during dances; others had to be hung from the ceiling of houses. In between were more conventional sizes intended to cover the faces or heads of the wearers. Purposes were as varied as sizes: they were shamanic, pantomimic and ceremonial (including a number of ludicrous and humorous masks) and totemic. The shamanic masks represented either spirits of the elements, places and inanimate things, or human or animal spirits that the shaman sought to subject to his will in order to become ever more powerful. The wearer was believed to become mysteriously imbued with the spirit of the mask he wore. Use of masks declined after the coming of the white man, as some of the customs associated with them died. In this respect, Christian influences were slight but disruptive.

Today, such economic factors as the opening of ore mines and the building of the Alaska pipeline, by luring the natives into more profitable occupations, make it seem highly unlikely that the native crafts that have survived can long continue.

BASKET-MAKING TRIBES OF BRITISH COLUMBIA (pp. 103–148)

The region of British Columbia inhabited by various tribes of the Salish was one of the principal basket-making areas of North America. From the forests and swamps of the area, the women gathered the raw materials for their craft, including the substances for dyeing grasses for decoration. A long tradition of basket making existed in this region, for baskets, bags and nets of all kinds were necessities to the food-gathering way of life of the people.

In decorating these baskets, the makers used two principal means of introducing a design in different-colored fibers as they coiled the basket. The simplest method was beading; a much more complex method was "imbrication," a technique which had a limited distribution and a sharp localization of pattern types. Baskets decorated in both methods, however, look very much the same in an illustration or reproduction. Basketry flourished where material was plentiful and the people led sedentary lives. Nomadic tribes often traded for baskets, giving dried meat, robes or other products in exchange, but even this practice waned after the introduction of metal pots as trade goods. Materials used were cedar bark dyed red, yellow and black, natural and dyed grass and black sedge bast. Local variations in color schemes were due to the availability or nonavailability of dyestuffs or materials. Only rarely was there any fixed connection between color and style; the principal aim of the designer was to obtain a contrast. Also, there was little effort to choose "natural" colors; panthers appeared on baskets as black, red, white or spotted. Certain exceptions to this rule were made: rain, hail and snow had certain specified colors. Natural dyes were eventually replaced by vivid commercial dyes.

Designs were partially traditional, partially individualistic. This led to many conflicting "interpretations" of designs. Often the same design had a whole flock of names applied by different makers, or the same idea would be expressed in numerous ways. As a rule the designs were geometric in form, as dictated by the method of weaving and decorating, although the inspiration for the design might be naturalistic. Again, as a rule, the earlier designs are geometric, while the more realistic figures are apt to be recent, often made with an eye to trade with the whites.

THE SOUTHWEST

The art of the inhabitants of the American Southwest, both of prehistoric and historic times, can be treated as a whole, for although decided differences exist—between peoples, areas and periods—there is a definite continuity between ancient and historic inhabitants of the area, often related in myths and legends, or semihistoric traditions, and testified to by similarities in culture and ways of life. One striking characteristic of the Pueblo behavior pattern of today is a great conservatism; this, coupled with comparative isolation until fairly recent times, in spite of Spanish military and religious conquest, accounts in great part for the longevity of Pueblo traditions and life styles. Part of the Pueblo culture as we know it is definitely aboriginal, though its germ may have originated elsewhere; no one Pueblo people living today is able to support satisfactorily a claim that it is ancestral to other tribes or to the culture as a whole outside a very limited area.

The Southwestern tradition centers on present-day Arizona and New Mexico, but includes portions of Utah, Colorado and Texas and part of Old Mexico as well. Just as a Woodland culture area and tradition developed in the eastern half of North America when the big-game hunting tradition ended (because of increasing desiccation of the land and the dying off of larger animals), a desert tradition developed in the area of the Plains region. Parts of the desert tradition—characterized by small bands of hunger-gatherers intensively exploiting all plant and animal resources, particularly seeds and grains, using baskets for hauling and storing foodstuffs, and metates and grindstones for pulverizing seeds and grains, even insects—survived until modern times. From this same tradition, but farther south in the area inhabited by ancient and modern Pueblo people, native agriculture—either assisted by irrigation or dependent upon trapped silt, flooded land or natural rainfall—made its appearance and became one of the definitive characteristics of this area. With agriculture came a completely sedentary way of life and the development of such arts as pottery and weaving. According to the most recent archaeological studies, the beginnings of pottery in the Southwest began about the start of the Christian era, roughly a millennium later than in the southeastern portion of North America. Pottery is certainly one of the most important of the arts of the area, because of its availability and the richness of its decoration, to say nothing of the information about kinship and migrations of people that can be obtained from studying its decorations. Weaving, though an ancient art in the area, is confined in this book to the comparatively recent art of the Navaho, working in sheep's wool introduced only after the Spanish conquest. Other areas of extremely specialized design are masks, katcinas and sand paintings.

The pottery of the various ancient Southwest cultures has much in common, and looks much the same to the untrained eye, though an expert can usually spot the origin of the piece by certain peculiarities of shape and design. As a rule, decoration is a better guide to identifying origin than

shape or technique; another general rule is, the older the ruin, the better the pottery. Pottery is the principal material found in the ruins; while types can be represented in a few forms, the decoration of each piece is virtually unique. The classes of pottery found in the ruins of the Southwest are much the same as those found in the mounds of the East, but vessels for holding water are more common. There is little to determine the age of much of this pottery, except to say that there is no evidence of Spanish influences, which probably means, however, that there was no apparent European intrusion, not that all of it predates the Conquest. Much ancient pottery decoration was derived from weaving techniques, most probably basketry. Geometrical designs are more simple, the most widely spread, and probably the most ancient. There is evidence of the evolution of complicated geometrical figures from simple forms. In fact, even the most complicated geometrical designs can be broken down into a few simple component elements; conversely, such combinations often came to be treated as design units themselves, and to be further combined into even more elaborate designs. Some of the geometric decoration from certain ruins, especially the more rectilinear, shows a Mexican rather than southwestern character, but there is nothing to connect any particular pueblo with the Aztec. Among the types of geometrical decoration found are terraced figures, spirals, frets, bands, dots, bars and zigzags. Each ruin has characteristic designs, with features peculiar to the locality. The geographical limits of each element of symbolism can be determined and information about migrations of clans obtained.

Examples of Hopi pottery decoration in this section extend from a period corresponding to the late middle ages in Europe to the mid-sixteenth century; designs shown were those used on pottery made at the pueblo of Sikyatki, near Old Walpi, abandoned about 1540; the influences of Sikyatki designs continued in the work of potters at other pueblos for over a century after the original pueblo was deserted. Some of the symbols used there recurred in Hopi legends and religion until modern times, and the designs themselves were revived by Hopi potters in the last decade of the nineteenth century. These decorations included life forms and mythological subjects, showing the awe which supernatural beings and their magic powers inspired in the minds of the makers. (Many of the pieces, incidentally, were used as—if not manufactured specifically for—mortuary offerings.) Most of the designs showed a love of detail and a delight in showing figures in motion. Few human figures were attempted, but many organs or parts of the human body occur separately. Among the symbolical designs, there is nothing that could serve as a time count, or that could be interpreted as calendric, hieroglyphic or phonic signs. Nor are there any records of any historic events. Other absent elements are katcina heads or masks; even quadrupeds are rare. There are, however, many winged figures—birds, bats, insects. Birds in particular are exceedingly rich in variety, and many kinds are depicted, but they are differentiated by highly conventionalized forms or feathers, so that it is difficult today to identify species. Another feature of Sikyatki decoration is "skybands," often with figures attached. Many of the life forms used are so conventionalized that identification is difficult or impossible. Geometrical designs are often quite elaborate, but can usually be reduced to a few elemental designs, usually rectilinear or rectangular. Curved lines are virtually absent, and there are few terraced designs or zigzags.

The designs from Zuñi pottery reproduced demonstrate the typically geometric character of that decoration. Elements used in building up these designs are triangles, open circles, coils, diamonds, scrolls, arches, meanders or Greek frets (these last two are found only in one particular kind of pottery). Zuñi pottery decoration used no vines or floral or checkered figures. There are some naturalistic designs, but few attempts to depict the human figure.

The southwestern United States, like the Northwest Coast, is one of the areas where the making and wearing of masks is of particular importance, both for the part such masks play in religious ceremonies and the opportunities for artistic expression. In 1879, when the Bureau of Ethnology was formed, no amount of money could have bought a genuine Zuñi mask or persuaded a tribesman to manufacture a false one, so thoroughly had the ex-treme exclusiveness of the Zuñi people preserved their strong individuality and regard for traditions. Less than two decades later, increased contact with whites had weakened both these traits to the point that it was possible to find unorthodox or unscrupulous men who would make anything for sale or trade. True ancestral masks are still guarded and used by Zuñi in their elaborate midwinter ceremonies. The masks of other Pueblo tribes often show Zuñi influence in shape and decoration; one distinguishing mark is the rolled collar of feathers or other material around the neck of the mask.

Most of the masks represent various katcinas, a word that has various meanings—either the supernatural beings personated by men, the mask and costume proper to such a personation, a doll or statuette carved to represent such a figure, or the ceremony in which dancers wearing the katcinas take part. As a rule, katcina masks are the property of individual clans that alone have the right to personate the spirits. There are a great number of katcinas among the Hopi, more than are ever personated at any one time, and the number is never constant. Katcinas "die out" as the clans who own them become extinct, though the masks may be inherited by other clans. New katcinas are adopted from various sources. In many cases, the same katcinas are known by different names, even within the same tribe. Decorations, color and ornaments of masks and costumes of katcinas are regarded as symbolic, and are usually easily recognized by Indians of the tribe. The masks of the katcinas are worn for many of the universal reasons (see the discussion of the Northwest Coast masks above), but in the pueblos they are also worn as disguises to prevent children who have not yet been initiated from knowing that the katcinas are actually men. (These masks were used literally as a disguise during the Pueblo Revolt of 1680, when many Indians wore their katcina masks so that they could not be identified by possible survivors.)

Certainly one of the best known of all American Indian art forms are the rugs and blankets woven by the Navaho. The Navaho learned the art from the Pueblo tribes with whom they came in contact at about the time Coronado made his first journey through the Southwest. Weaving was learned even more recently than this, perhaps about two hundred years ago, but the Navaho quickly surpassed their teachers. They spun and wove only in wool. The raw wool was washed only after shearing, then carded and spun by hand. Some of the dyes used were made from vegetable sources, some traded for from the Mexicans or the Americans. A bright red color was provided by unraveling bayeta, a fine grade of red trade cloth supplied from Mexico. Toward the end of the nineteenth century, purchased aniline dyes were introduced, as were manufactured yarns from the States. The rugs and blankets featured geometric or highly conventionalized designs, usually of comparatively simple design and large scale; designs on belts and sashes, also geometric, were considerably more complex. The rugs were woven from the bottom up on an upright loom. At times, when especial care was being taken to ensure regularity of pattern at each end, a portion of the top would be woven next to correspond with the bottom, then the center was completed. The blankets were in single ply, with the same design on both sides. Usually the design would be worked out only in the head of the weaver; for a particularly complicated and important pattern, the design was sometimes drawn out on the sand.

Another specialized form of southwestern art was the "sand painting" used in various shamanic practices, such as the Mountain Chant, or the healing ritual of the Navaho. Many of these ceremonies were ordered and paid for by individuals, and could be very costly, for they included the services not only of a priest but of several artists who raced to complete elaborate sand paintings within the space of one dawn-to-dusk day, and often special grinders who prepared colors, as well. The colors were symbolical and were of natural origin, such as various colors of sand or types of crushed rock. These paintings, at times quite large in size, combined geometrical designs, often symbolical, with highly conventionalized life forms, likewise of a mythological character. Most of the sand paintings illustrated were done by the Navaho, who derived their ideas of technique from Pueblo tribes, but drew their figures from Navaho mythology. These paintings are supposed to represent ancient paintings done by the gods on clouds. Other examples of sand paintings were done by members of the Sia (or Tsia), a once numerous Pueblo tribe reduced to just over a hundred members in 1890. Though nominally converts to the Roman Catholic religion, they still performed many of their traditional ceremonies, and all important events—baptism, marriage, funerals—were usually celebrated dually with both pagan and Christian rites.

PREHISTORIC ART
OF THE
EASTERN WOODLANDS

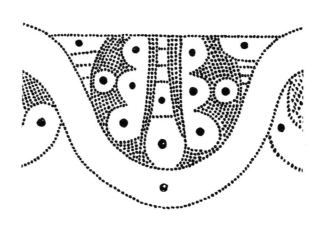

A: One of the rather scarce examples of vases shaped like a human head, perhaps for mortuary use, from a mound near Pecan Point, Arkansas. B: An exceptionally fine example of a human effigy in pottery from the Middle Mississippi Valley Group; the body is painted, but the figure wears only a necklace.

Bowls of the Middle Mississippi Valley Group found in Arkansas, with realistic or grotesque heads of birds, frogs or animals modeled in the round and applied.

A: Owl-shaped bottle found in Arkansas. B: Long-necked bottle with three human heads found in Georgia. C: "Triune" vase (very similar to B) found near the Cumberland River, Tennessee. D, F, G: Examples of vases with realistic or grotesque heads of humans or birds. E: Vase with fluted sides found in Arkansas.

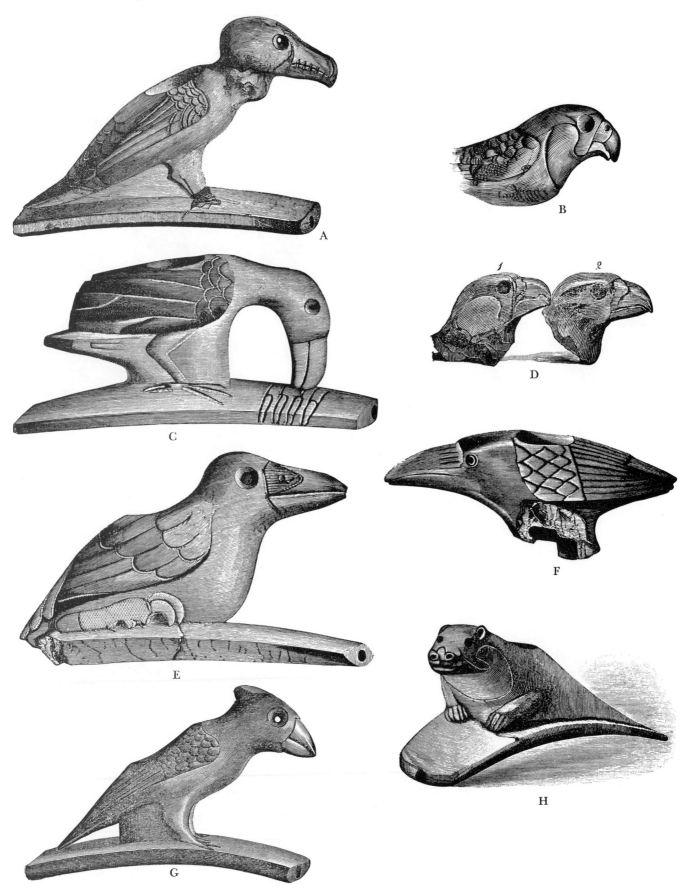

Bird and animal effigies carved on pipes found in mounds, identified tentatively. A: Turkey buzzard. B: Hawk. C: Wading bird. D: Hawks. E: Woodpecker. F: Crow or raven. G: Cardinal. H: Otter.

Pipes from mounds. A: Hawk. B, D, F, H: Human heads, some of the finest specimens known. C: Bat (?). E: Otter (?). G: Bird monster with human head.

A: Stone pipe from Hollywood mound, Georgia, which recalls the kneeling hunchbacked figures found in pottery. B: Image pipe found in mound near Clarendon, Arkansas. C: Cup from the Southern Appalachian Group, decorated with horned or antlered rattlesnake. D: Bowl from mound in Mackintosh County, Georgia, decorated with engraved lines and carving.

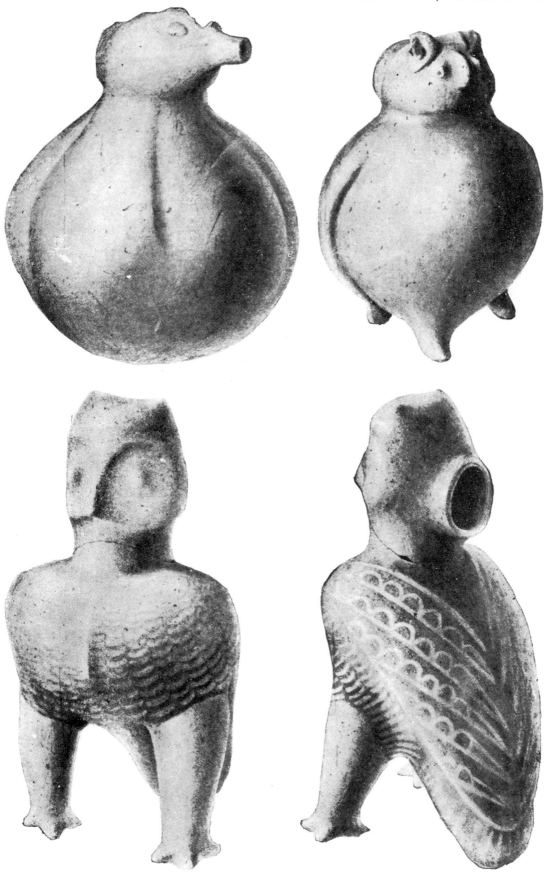

Bird vessels from the Middle Mississippi Valley Group, showing treatment of bird forms by ancient potters. The owl vessel (below, two views) recalls painted owl vessels of the Rio Colorado in the Southwest.

A: Long-necked bottle of eccentric form from Franklin County, Alabama. B: Painted design on the preceding, in red and white on gray. C: Bottle from Arkansas. D: Engraved design on the preceding, with winged and crested serpent and sunflowers (?). E: Long-necked bottle with unusual decoration from Pecan Point, Arkansas. F: Bottle from Arkansas with engraved design of linked scrolls often associated with reptiles.

A: Long-necked bottle from Georgia, resembling bottles from Tennessee or the Middle Mississippi Valley Group. B, D: Two long-necked bottles with painted decoration of red on yellowish paste from the Middle Mississippi Valley Group. C: Bottle from the Middle Mississippi Valley Group with decoration in color.

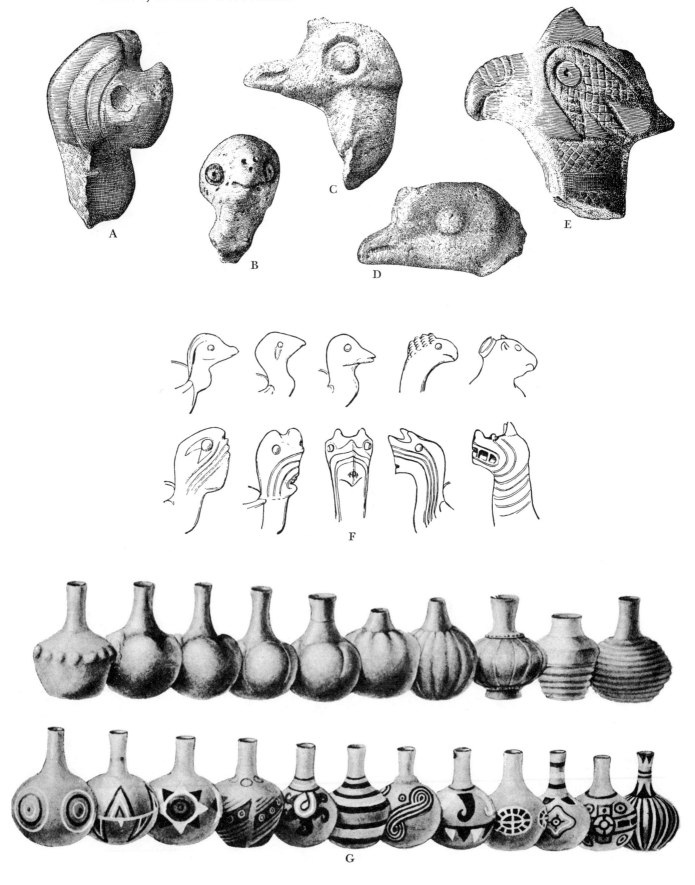

A—F: Realistic and grotesque heads of birds modeled in the round and applied to vases, from mounds of the Middle Mississippi Valley Group. G: Elaborations on typical long-necked bottles with examples of molded, incised and painted decoration typical of the Middle Mississippi Valley Group.

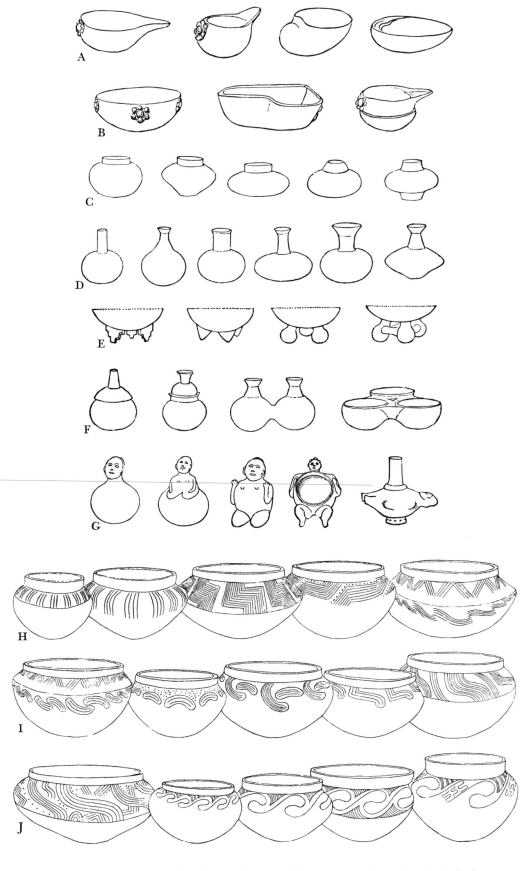

Shapes of pottery typical of the Middle Mississippi Valley Group. Rows A & B: Imitations of shells. D: Long-necked bottles. E: Bowls on tripods. F: Rare compound forms. G: Human effigies adapted to bottle forms. H, I, J: Vessels, mostly for cooking, of the Gulf Coast Group, from Perdido Bay, Florida, with varied ornaments incised on rim and neck.

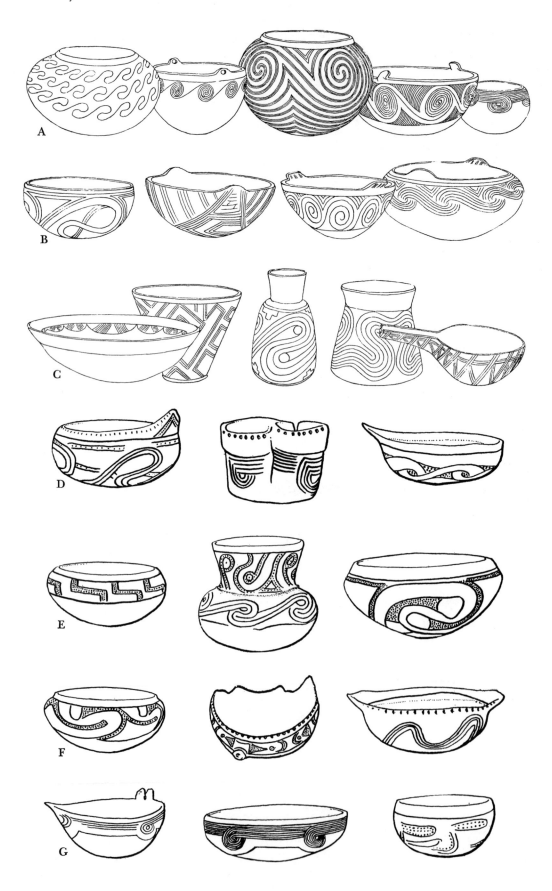

Vessels of the Gulf Coast Group. A–C: From Perdido Bay, Florida. Many show evidence of having been used in fires, indicating they were cooking vessels. D–G: Vessels from Walton's Camp, Choctawhatchee Bay, Florida. Several show imitations of shell forms.

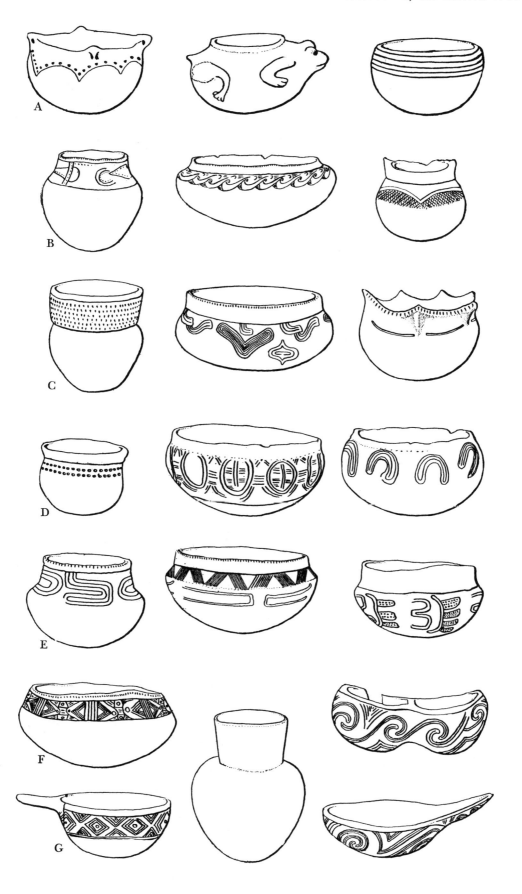

A: Three vessels from Walton's Camp, Choctawhatchee Bay, Florida, one modeled in a frog shape. B–G: Other vessels from the Gulf Coast Group, also found in Florida, with various types of incised decoration on necks and rims.

Decorative elements used on pottery of the Middle Mississippi Valley Group, usually applied in red and white paint. Many of the designs are undoubtedly symbolic, and include cross and sun shapes.

Variations of cross designs found on Mound Builder art, carved on shells and stones, scratched on copper plates, and painted on pottery in many of the areas once occupied by Mound Builders.

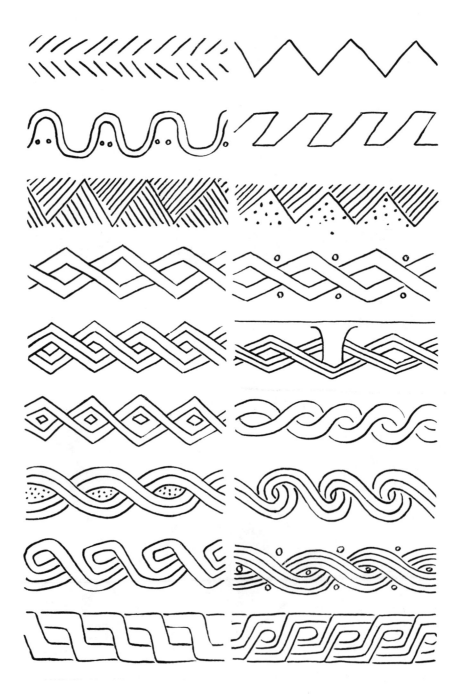

Incised decorations on earthenware of the Ohio Valley Group of Mound Builders, usually found applied to the neck and lip of vases. Some elements of the design suggest introductions from southern peoples.

Incised and molded designs occurring on Iroquoian earthenware, which is found from the area around Chesapeake Bay north to Canada. Pieces in the group illustrated came from West Virginia, Pennsylvania and New York State.

More designs from Iroquoian pottery, showing the linear simplicity of typical designs from the Wilkes-Barre region of Pennsylvania.

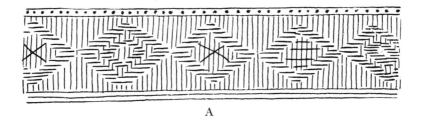

A

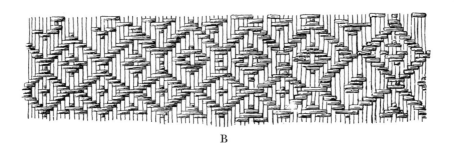

B

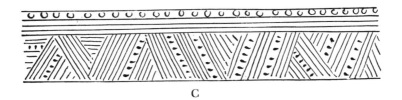

C

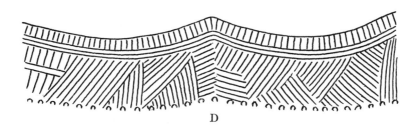

D

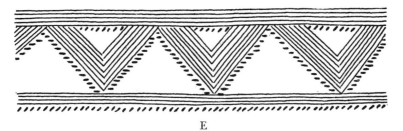

E

Incised designs on Iroquoian Group pottery from the Wyoming Valley of Pennsylvania. Figure B, a design taken from Cherokee basketwork, shows the probable derivation of incised design A from basketry.

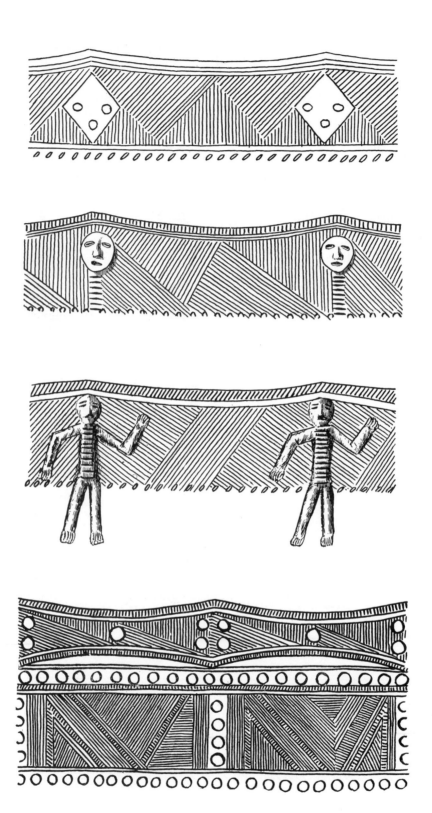

Incised, molded and applied decorations on pottery of the Iroquoian Group. At the bottom: a double zone of design applied to the rim of a vessel.

Stamp designs restored from impressions on vases of the Southern Appalachian Group.
Decorations formed by the application of such elaborately figured stamps to wet clay were
typical of Southern Appalachian pottery, but rarely used elsewhere except in Central and
South America.

Engraved designs from pottery of the Southern Appalachian Group. A: Human head or mask entwined in a conventionalized rattlesnake form. This face is unique in pottery, though similar to human faces found engraved on sheet copper or shell.

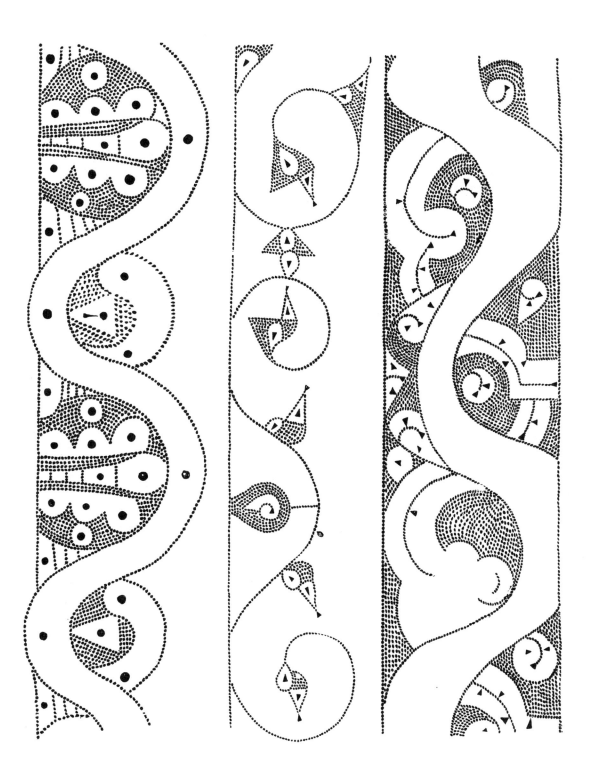

Engraved designs from pottery of the Gulf Coast Group found at Tarpon Springs, Florida. The elaborate curving designs are worked out with innumerable punched indentations, giving a "tattoo" effect.

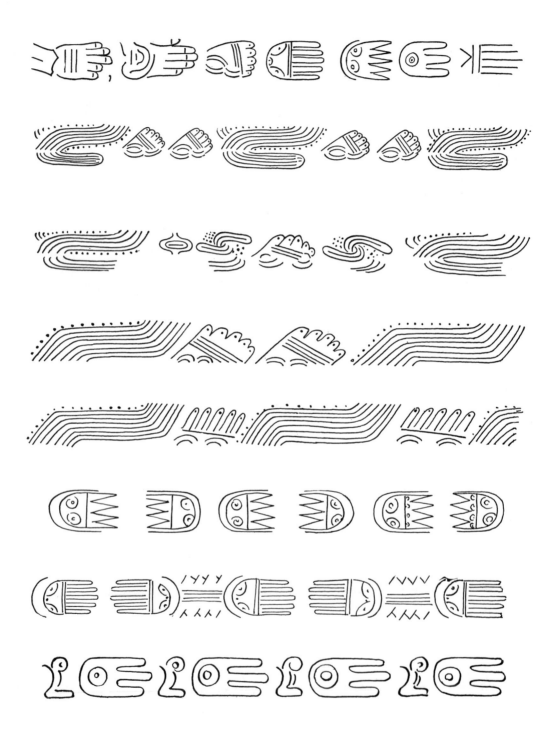

Designs from pottery of the Gulf Coast Group found on the coasts of Alabama and Florida, featuring purely conventionalized designs and more or less fully conventionalized life forms.

Purely conventionalized designs found engraved on the pottery of the Gulf Coast Group from Alabama and Florida.

Variations of the "frog concept" found on pottery of the Gulf Coast Group recovered from sites on the coast of Florida.

Variations of the "bird concept" in Gulf Coast Group pottery found on the Florida coast. Such conventionalized representations of birds are often found on pots bearing a head of a bird modeled in relief.

Designs from the Middle Mississippi Valley Group, featuring elaborate meanders, scrolls and twined designs.

Incised designs from vases of the Lower Mississippi Valley Group of Mound Builders. The decorations were engraved with great regularity and precision on the polished sides of vessels.

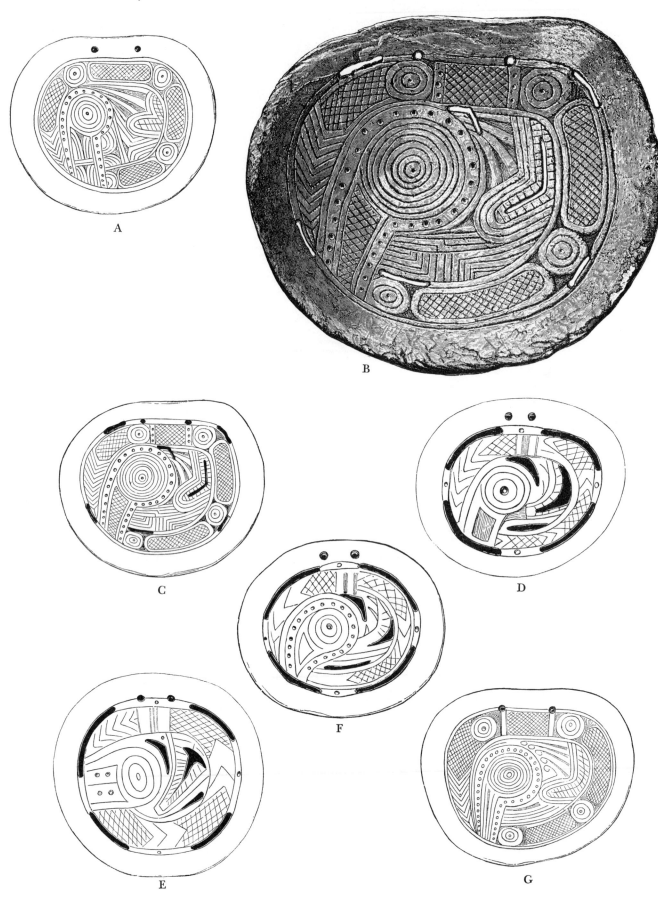

Shell gorgets from various mounds, with conventionalized rattlesnake designs. B shows an actual photograph of the gorget rendered in C. All the renderings show the holes by which the gorgets were originally attached to garments or breast coverings.

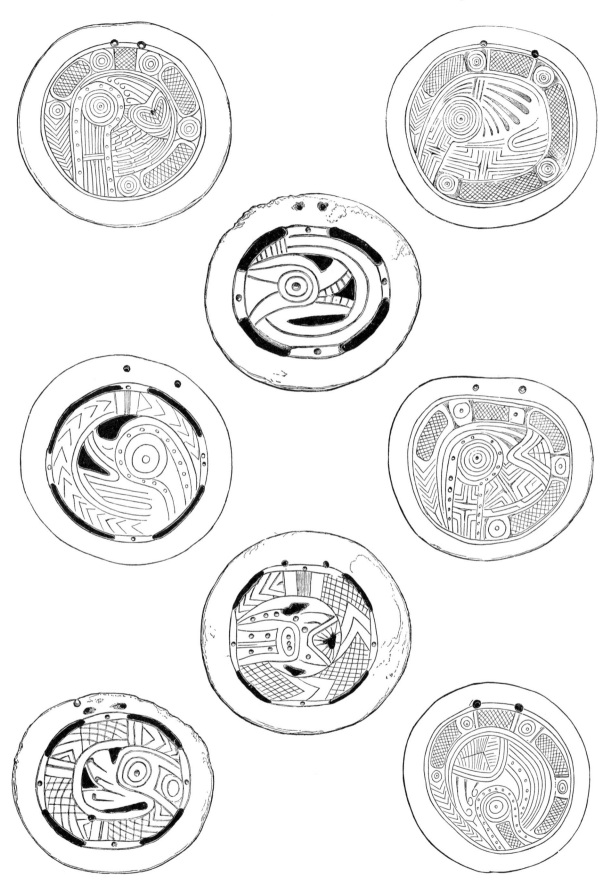

Gorgets from mounds in Tennessee. In the designs, the spots and scales of the snakes are conventionalized, and eyes are usually shown as concentric circles. The rattlesnakes are shown coiled with the head in the center of the circle formed by the body.

A, B: Winged human figures engraved on two copper plates from Etowah Mound, Georgia. Both figures are carrying severed human heads. C, E, F, G: Human figures on shell gorgets from mounds in Tennessee and Missouri. D: Stone disk from Carthage, Alabama, with conventionalized serpent and human hand.

A–C: Designs on plates made by Mound Builders, found in Tennessee, featuring "equal-arm crosses" or "four world-quarter" designs in the centers. Such designs are found on pottery, stone, copper and shell in mounds in Tennessee, Alabama, Georgia, Mississippi and Arkansas. D–F: Highly conventionalized bird designs on shell gorgets from Tennessee.

A–D: Spider designs on gorgets from mounds in Missouri, Illinois and Tennessee. E–I: Scalloped shell disks from Tennessee. These are perhaps conventionalized sun disks; some (F, G, I) have spiral centers.

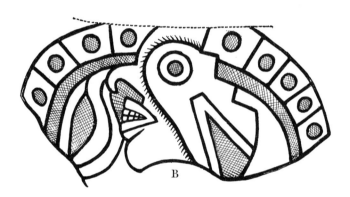

A: Eagle from a copper plate found by Major James Powell in a mound near Peoria, Illinois. B, C: Eagle and "eagle-man mask" from a vase of the Gulf Coast Group found at Jolly Bay, Florida.

THE EASTERN WOODLANDS
IN THE
HISTORIC PERIOD

A

B

Two mid-nineteenth-century drawings by Iroquois Indians. A: Illustration of one of
the myths that were centered around Atotarho, based, like Hiawatha, on an historical
figure, but one who was so cruel and cunning he was regarded as a wizard. B: Pictograph
entitled "Returning Thanks to the Great Spirit." Ideas like the Great Spirit and the
Happy Hunting Ground were developed in Indian religion in response to ideas introduced by Christian missionaries.

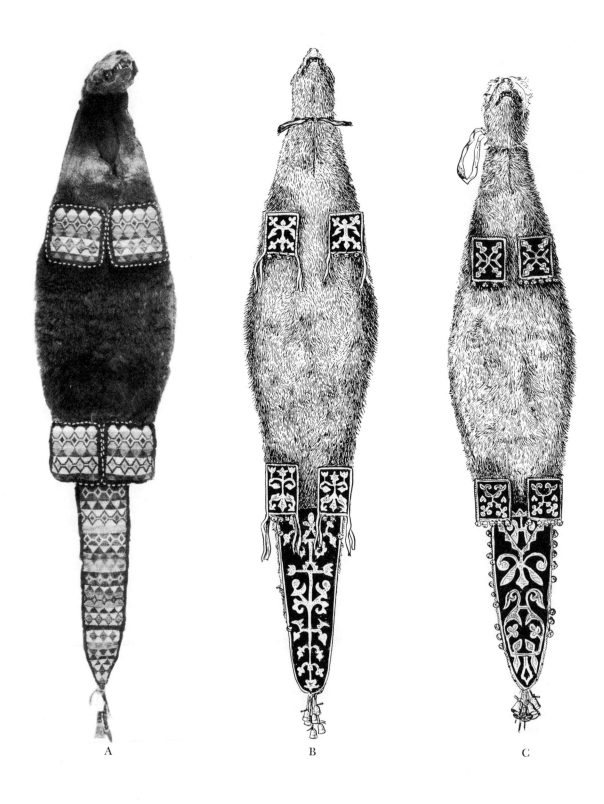

A   B   C

Examples of Winnebago beading. A: Dance pouch made from the skin of an entire otter, with beading in diamond shapes. B, C: Pouches also made of whole otter skins, but decorated with curving floral designs on cloth, influenced by the needlework taught in Canadian convents by Roman Catholic sisters.

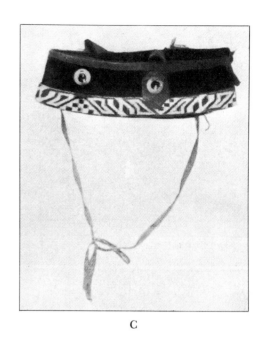

A   B

C

D   E   F

A–C: Winnebago beaded work showing both the old traditional geometric patterns and the bolder geometric and floral patterns of the later period. D: Woman's moccasin. F: Man's moccasin. These show the different shapes adapted for the sexes, though both are decorated with similar patterns in traditional geometric beadwork. E: Woman's moccasin with silk appliqué work, another example of white influences and trade materials.

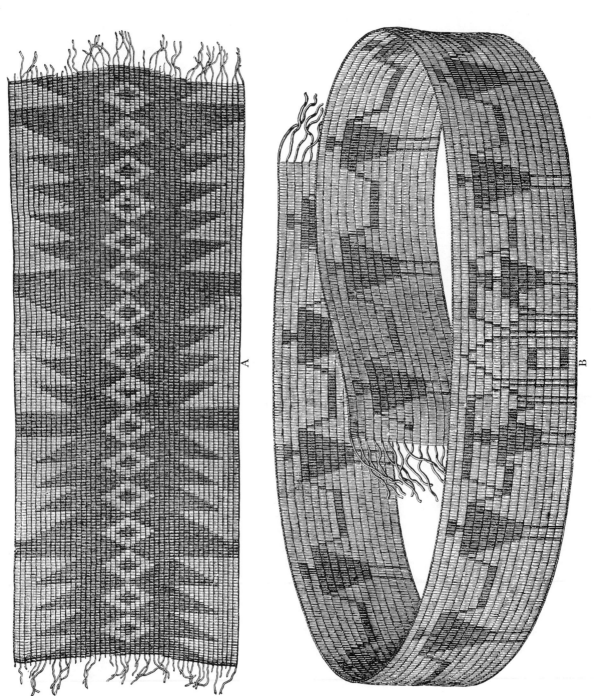

A: Onondaga wampum belt in almost perfect condition, 45 rows wide and 240 rows long. B: One of the very finest wampum belts, an Onondaga example containing almost 10,000 beads. It may have represented the founding of the Iroquoian League and perhaps records a treaty between the tribe and the U.S. government. An Indian tradition said the belt was made by George Washington.

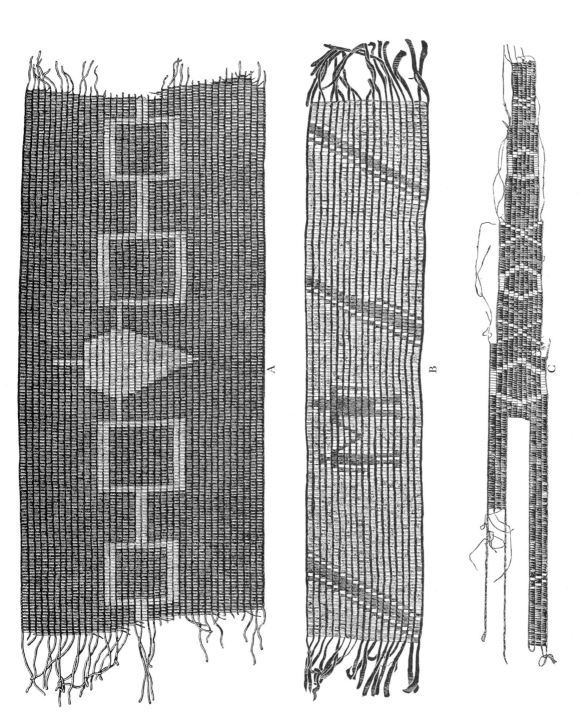

A: Onondaga belt said to be very old and to represent the formation of the Iroquoian League, its design meaning "one heart for all the nations." But the beads are too regular to be handmade. B: The Penn belt, believed to be the one delivered by the Lenni Lenape to William Penn at the time of the celebrated treaty at Shackamaxon in 1682. It remained in the possession of the Penn family till the mid-nineteenth century. C: Mohawk belt of unusual form, adapted to some particular, but unknown, use. The beads are irregular but new-looking.

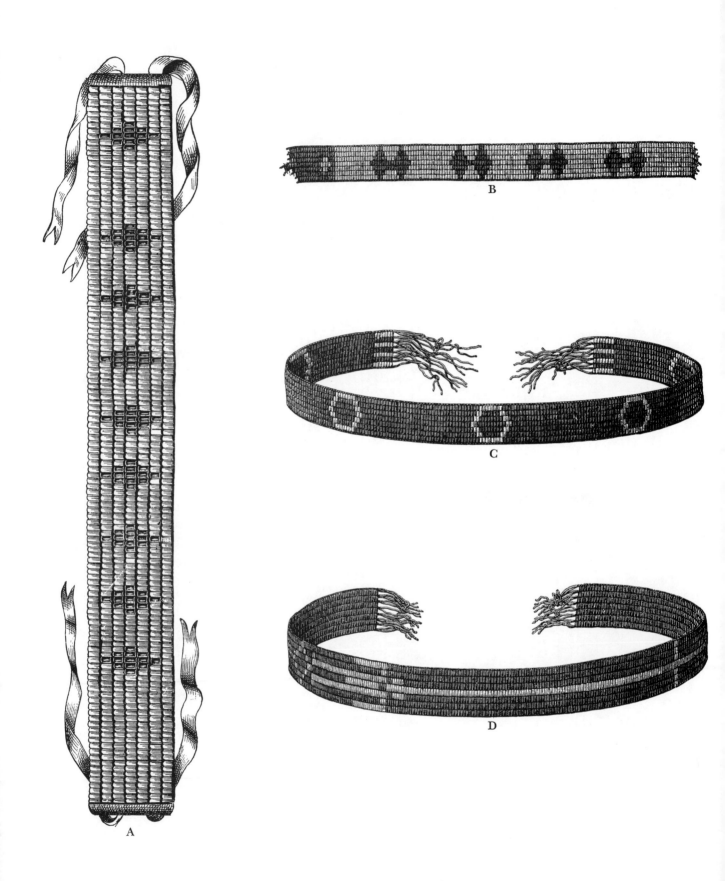

A: Mohawk belt, probably ca. 1850–60 but made of old beads once belonging to Joseph Brant. B–D: Onondaga belts. B is fragmentary; C may refer to a treaty; D, which is pictographic, was acquired in perfect condition, though quite old. This last belt may have been made for the French.

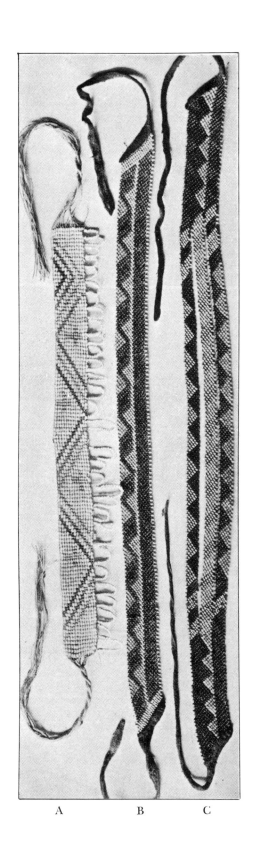

A B C   D   E

A–C: Menominee necklaces showing simple designs using triangles and zigzags. D, E: Beaded garters, also Menominee, with elaborate designs based on diamond and trapezoidal shapes.

Woven bags used for storing dried food, with old Winnebago designs. A: Deer and thunderbird. B: Thunderbird. C: Geometric design. The animal designs may be property marks.

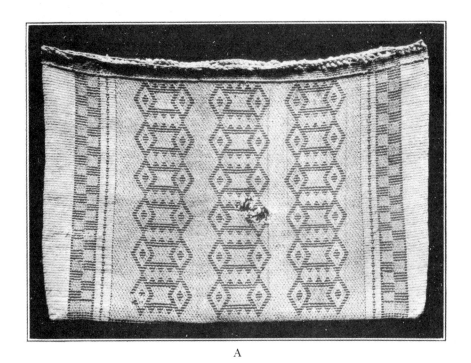

A

B   C   D   E   F   G   H   I   J

A: Winnebago woven bag for storing food, decorated with geometric design of diamond shapes and triangles. B–J: Winnebago beaded belts and cross belts. D, E and F show old-fashioned traditional designs of small understated geometric shapes, while the others show later designs in floral and bold geometric patterns.

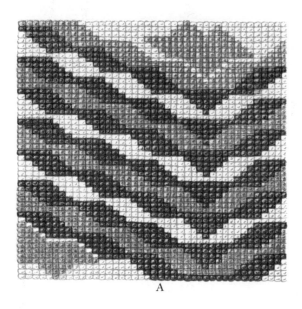

A, B: Dancing garters with beaded designs, worn by members of the once powerful Midé or Grand Medicine society. These garters, tied below each knee, were an essential part of the elaborate dance and ceremonial costumes of the Ojibwas. C: Menominee woven bag with geometric design, intended for storing food.

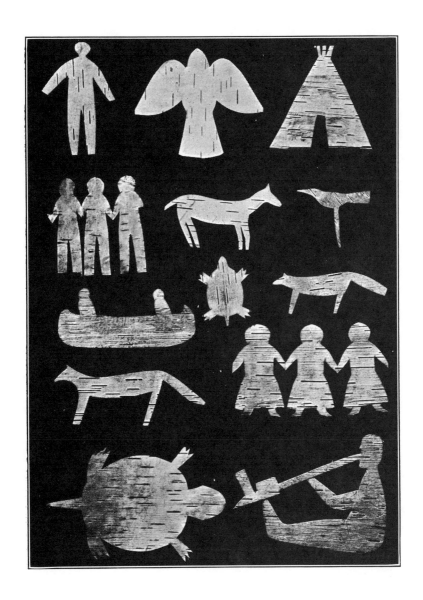

Birchbark transparencies made by Woodlands tribes, some merely for pleasure, some intended as patterns for beading designs.

More birchbark transparencies made by Woodlands tribes. These are beading designs. Formerly the designs were pricked out with a fishbone, then cut with scissors, without first tracing the outline.

THE PLAINS AREA

Indian pictograph of the battle of the Little Bighorn, drawn by Red Horse, a Sioux Chief who was prominent in the engagement. The drawing shows the victorious warriors leaving the battlefield with their captured horses wearing military saddles.

Another pictograph of the battle of the Little Bighorn. This shows the Sioux slain in the battle. Each of the dead would be easily identifiable by their tribesmen through details of dress, paint and adornment.

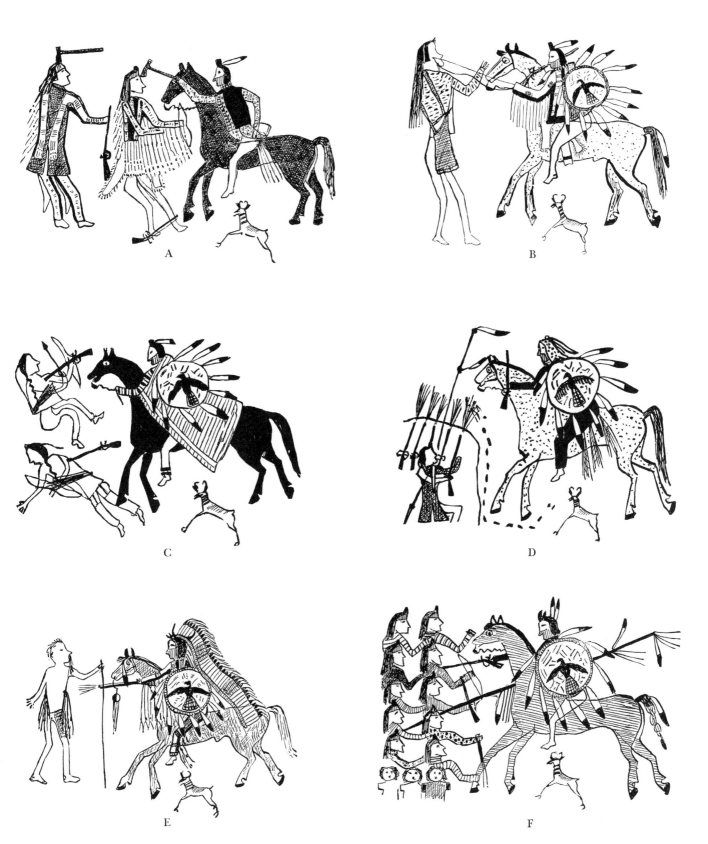

Pages from the pictographic autobiography of Running Antelope, chief of the Uncpapa Dakotas (Sioux). Drawn at Grand River, Dakota Territory, in 1873, this narrative shows him killing various groups of people. A: Two Arikara chiefs (in 1856). B: An Arikara (1857). C: Two Arikara hunters (1859). D: Five Arikaras (1863). E: An Arikara (1853). F: Ten men and three squaws (1856). Running Antelope's signature appears at the bottom of each drawing.

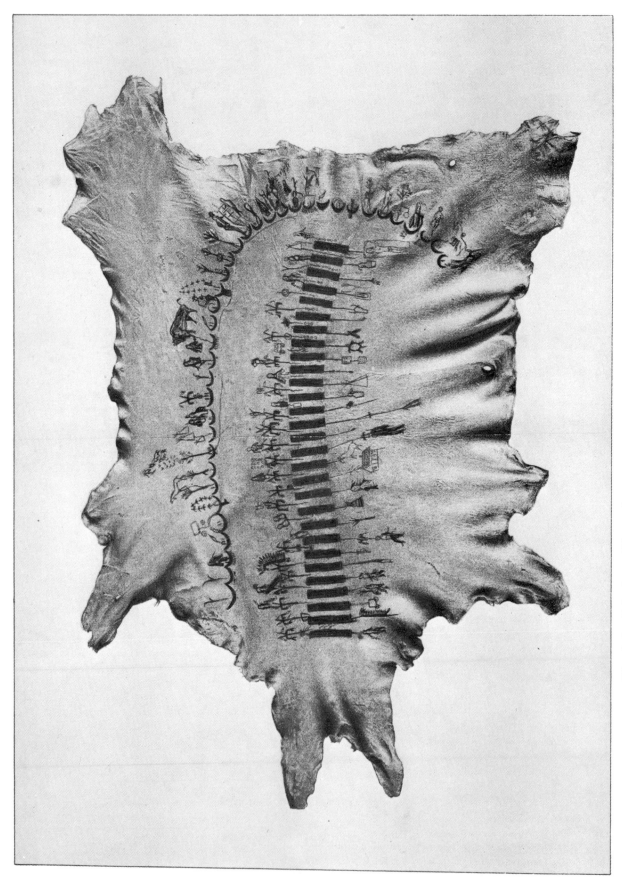

The Anko Calendar, a Kiowa piece. The pictographs attached to the bars in the center form a winter count, while the drawings attached to the crescent shapes around the outer edge give a monthly history of 37 months' duration in the 1890s.

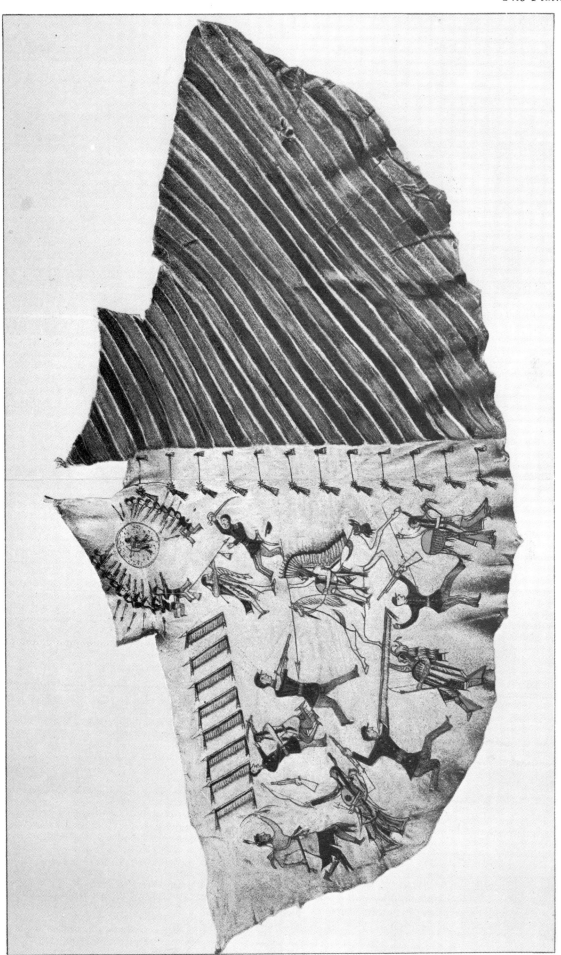

The Do-giagya-guat, or Battle Tipi (tipi with battle pictures) of the Kiowas. This is a small buckskin replica of a noted heraldic tipi that burned in the winter of 1872-73. On one side it is decorated with a pattern of stripes, on the other with a pictographic representation of encounters with United States soldiers.

Apache medicine shirt, with designs painted on buckskin. The symbolism of each shirt was individual and unique, not traditional, and each shirt was necessarily different. Among the Apaches, the buckskin used for such ceremonial purposes (shirts, masks, drums and so forth) had to be taken from a stranded animal that was strangled to death, and not shot.

This Apache medicine shirt is made of an entire deerskin with a slit in the center for the head, so that the piece may be worn like a poncho. Although each shirt was different in design, certain typical symbols constantly reappear: sun, moon, stars, rainbows, lightning, smoke clouds, hail, tarantulas, centipedes, snakes and representations of the gods.

A

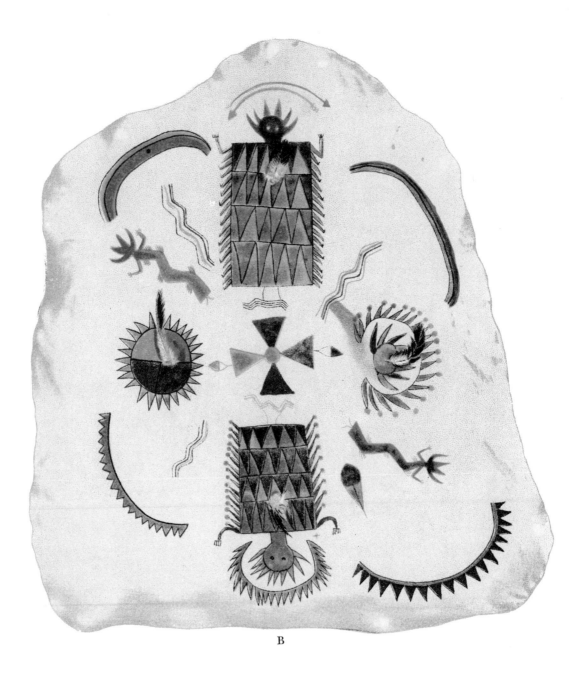

B

A: Apache medicine sash, used to bind the kilt during medicine dances. Its symbolism was similar to that of the medicine shirt. Once he donned his regalia, the Apache medicine man ceased to be an individual, and became the power he represented. B: Another Apache medicine shirt.

Two pictographs drawn by an Indian prisoner at St. Augustine, Florida. A: Buffalo hunt. The dashed lines represent footprints. B: Wrestling match between two Indians. A hunter standing by offers a turkey to the winner of the match.

Pictographic roster of heads of families in the band of Chief Big Road of the Ogalala Sioux, obtained at Standing Rock Reservation in 1883 for the purpose of taking a census of the people requiring distribution of food and clothing. Each Indian is identified by a pictograph representing his name. This is the band of Low Dog, who is shown at the upper left.

Another page from the Ogalala roster. Shown here is the band of The Bear Spares Him, who is shown at the upper left. Other names given are Fears Nothing (top row, second from right), Kills Crows [the Indians] (top row, far right), Red Earth Woman (bottom row, second from right) and Carries the Badger (middle of bottom row).

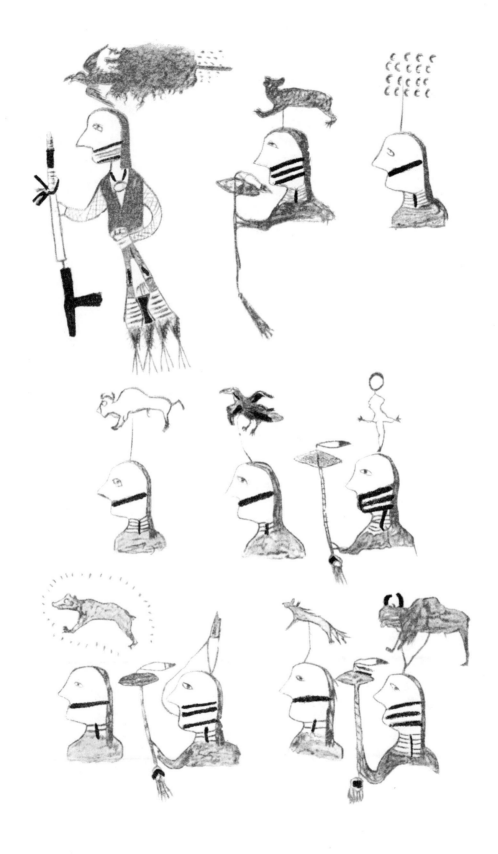

From the Ogalala roster: the band of subchief Big Road, who is shown at the upper left, distinguished by the pipe and bag shown near him. The style of face painting worn by each head of a family is carefully given in this roster.

Various styles of tipi decoration employed by the Sioux in the nineteenth century. Tipi decoration might be dictated by a personal "mystery" or "medicine," or else the ornaments might contain references to the clan or subgens to which the owner belonged. For instance, the tipi at the lower right belonged to a member of the Black Bear subgens. The circle at the top represented a bear's lair, the next band lightning, then a design of bear's claws.

Any Indian skilled in reading the symbolism of tipi decoration would be able to decipher, or at any rate guess, the meanings behind the various decorations of these tipis. He would know, for instance, that A was owned by a member of the Pipe subgens of the Sioux and that C was owned by a man who had danced the pipe dance three times, while the owner of D had danced the pipe dance four times.

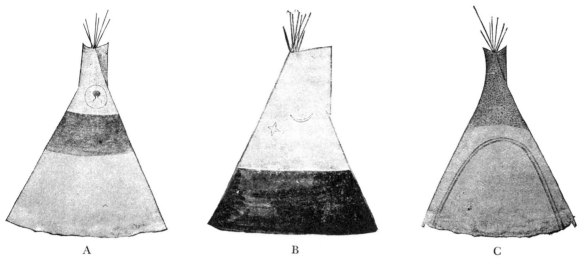

A   B   C

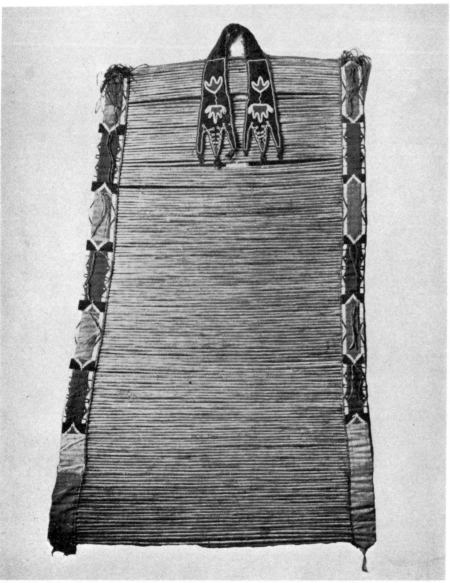

D

Other examples of decorated tipis. B: The decoration represents night and the moon and a star. C: Omaha tipi decorated with a rainbow. D: Arapaho bed, one of the few articles of furniture to be found in a Plains tipi. It is composed of willow slats joined together, and ornamented with beadwork. Only the headpiece, or backrest, of the actual bed is shown here.

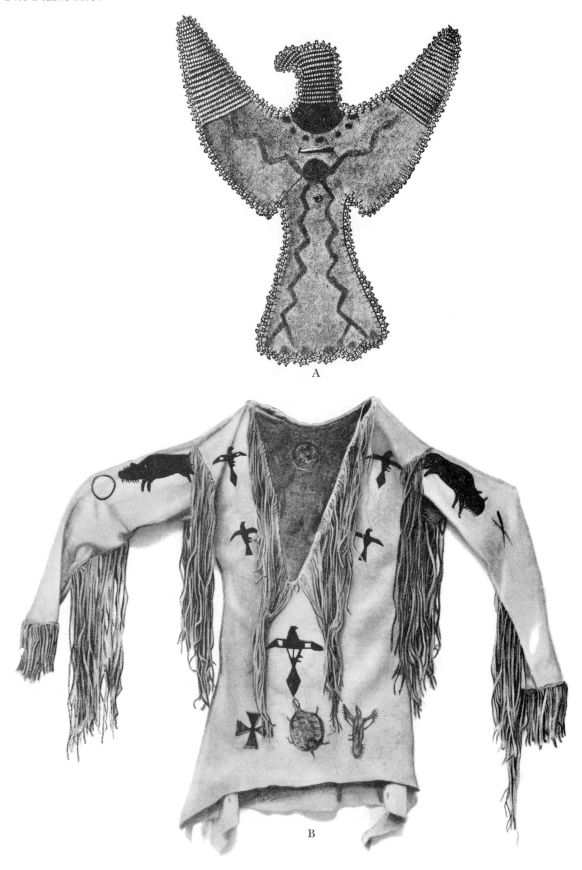

A: Thunderbird, cut from rawhide and decorated with beads. Such ornaments were frequently worn on the forehead by dancers. Possibly Arapaho. B: Arapaho "ghost shirt,"
worn by participants in the Ghost Dance religion. The symbolic designs all had reference
to particular portions of this religion. Wearers of these shirts thought they would prove
invulnerable to the bullets of the white soldiers.

THE NORTHWEST COAST, ALASKA AND THE ARCTIC REGIONS

Tlingit hats and shamanic masks. A: Killer whale, an animal claimed as a totem by a number of Tlingit clans. B—E: Masks belonging to a shaman at Alsek River, named Weasel Wolf. B represents a spirit called Cross-man. C is a "spirit-put-on-mask" (put on in time of war). D is a raven. E is a "land-otter man-spirit."

Northwest Coast masks. A: Maskette collected from the Makah Indians at Neeah Bay, but probably made by the Vancouver Islanders. B, C: Profile and front views of a dancing mask, shaped like a bird's head with movable lower jaw, from the Bellabella Indians of British Columbia. D: Profile and full-face view of a dancing helmet of the same origin as A. This shows possibly a combination animal. E, F: Profile and top view of a Haida killer-whale mask collected at the Klemahoon village, Prince of Wales Island, Alaska.

Northwest Coast masks. A: Dancing mask of the Bellabella Indians of British Columbia. Probably a festival rather than a shamanic mask, it is carved of Alaska cedar. Parts of the painted surface are covered with powdered mica. B: Dancing mask (Haida?), incomplete and never used. It has neither air nor eye holes, and may have been made for sale to tourists as a curiosity. The tiara of bear claws is most unusual. C: Mask from the Northwest Coast collected by the Wilkes expedition in the 1840s. Made of Alaska cedar, the face is painted black with bits of mica applied to the surface. D: Dancing mask from the Northwest Coast collected by the Wilkes expedition. E: Mask of wood with bits of animal skin glued on for hair and beard.

A,B: Dancing masks of the type carved on Vancouver Island, then sold to the Makah Indians of Cape Flattery, who painted them according to their own wishes. C: Another dancing mask used by the Makah Indians of Cape Flattery, Washington, in various ceremonies about which little is known. D: Dancing mask used by the Makah tribe, Cape Flattery. E: Innuit maskette from St. Paul, Kodiak Island, made by the Kaniagmut Eskimo after an ancient model. F: Shamanic mask representing a lynx or wildcat, a mythical animal spirit which has appeared to the shaman during his meditations.

A

B

C

A: Northwest Coast maskette made by the Tlingit Indians of Sitka. Carved of wood with pieces of shell glued on, the maskette represents an otter and frog, and belonged to a shaman. B: Mask collected by the Wilkes expedition in the mid-nineteenth century. Made of birchwood decorated with paint and haliotis shell, the carving represents the beaver totem. C: Wooden drum with a design of a killer whale, made by the Tlingit tribe.

Designs on a large Tsimshian box for keeping blankets, an important form of wealth among the Northwest Coast tribes. Woodwork was especially elaborately decorated by this tribe, with every surface of the box entirely covered with animal forms, often greatly distorted to make them fit into the given area.

A: Large copper plate of the Tsimshian. Made originally of native copper, later of imported metals, these plates represented enormous sums in terms of blankets, skins, barrels of oil and so forth, as distributed in intertribal trading, and were used only at important potlaches (gift-giving ceremonies). B: Tsimshian hat made of spruce-root basketry with a painted design. While the design of the hat and the basketry technique are simple, the decoration is quite elaborate.

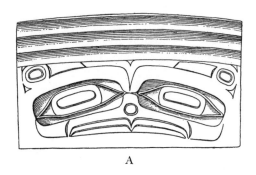

A

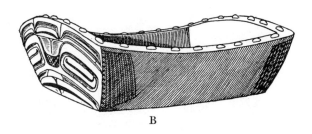

B

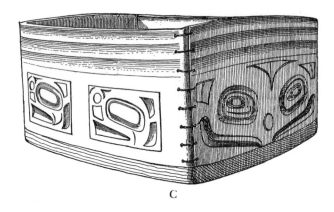

C

D

E

Tsimshian art. A, C: Box made of thin planks of wood steamed and bent into shape. The planks were sewn with cedar twigs and fastened to a wooden bottom with pegs. B: Food tray made of a large block of wood hollowed out. D: Stone mortar, with a design of an animal face. E: Leggings, with geometrical designs worked in porcupine quills. Among the Tsimshian geometrical designs were less common than those based on realistic forms.

A

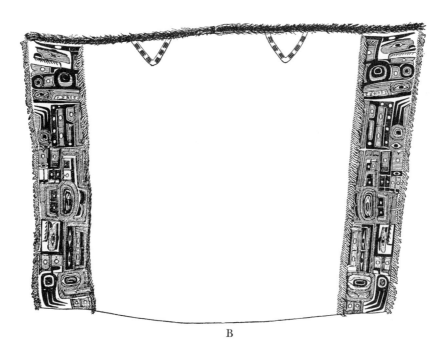

B

A: Tsimshian skin apron with painted decoration and quilled embroidery. The painted animal forms are realistic, while the embroidery designs are geometric. B: Tsimshian painted skin blanket, part of the traditional costume of members of this tribe.

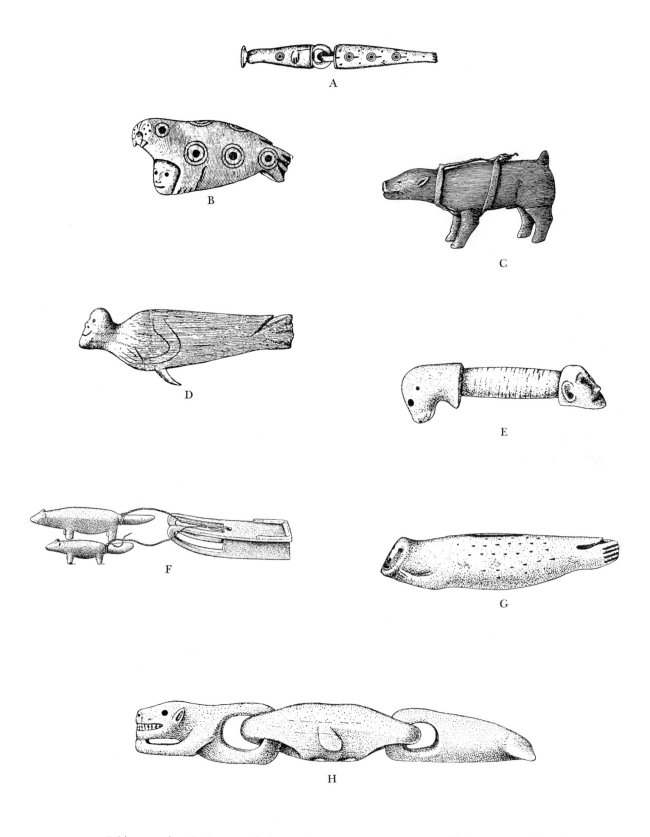

Eskimo carvings in ivory, made for various uses; some represent realistic, some mythic animals or a combination of both. A: Seal with a mouth like a lamprey. B: Walrus spirit with a human face on its breast. C: Toy bear with dog harness. D: Mermaid-like creature. E: Float with human and animal heads. F: Toy dogs with sled. G: Cord handle from Sledge Island with a mermaid-like creature, half seal, half human. H: Ivory cord handle in the form of a creature half whale, half white bear.

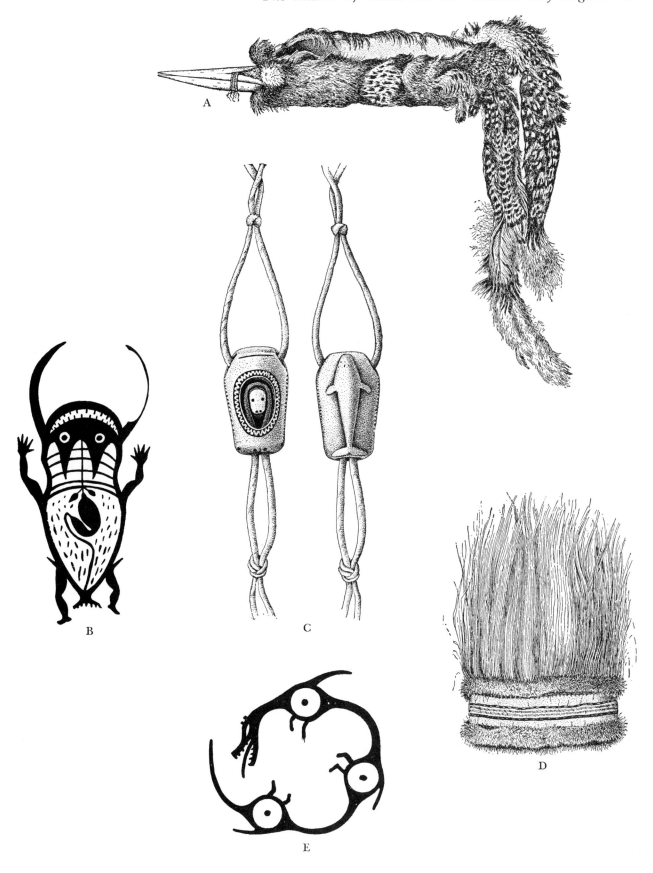

A: Fillet from Ikogmut, lower Yukon, used in dances. B: Drawing of an Eskimo mythic creature believed to be invisible to all but shamans. C: Obverse and reverse of an Eskimo cord attacher, made of ivory and carved with figures of seal and whale. D: Fillet from lower Yukon, made of sealskin and reindeer skin. E: Drawing of the *pal-rai-yuk* in a wooden tray. This was an Eskimo mythic creature something like a crocodile.

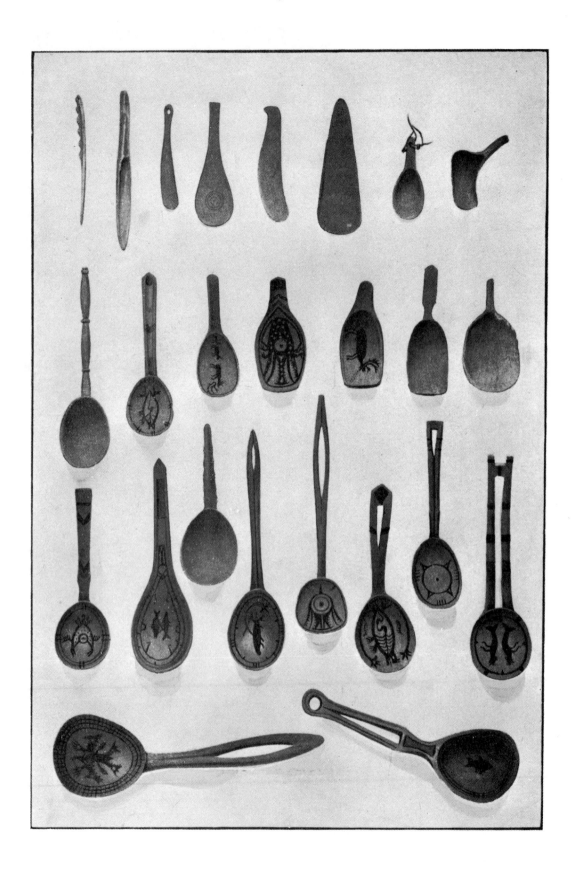

Eskimo spoons and ladles from the lower Yukon and Norton Sound areas, showing various shapes and forms of handles and types of decoration. The animal forms painted on the bowls are both realistic and mythic.

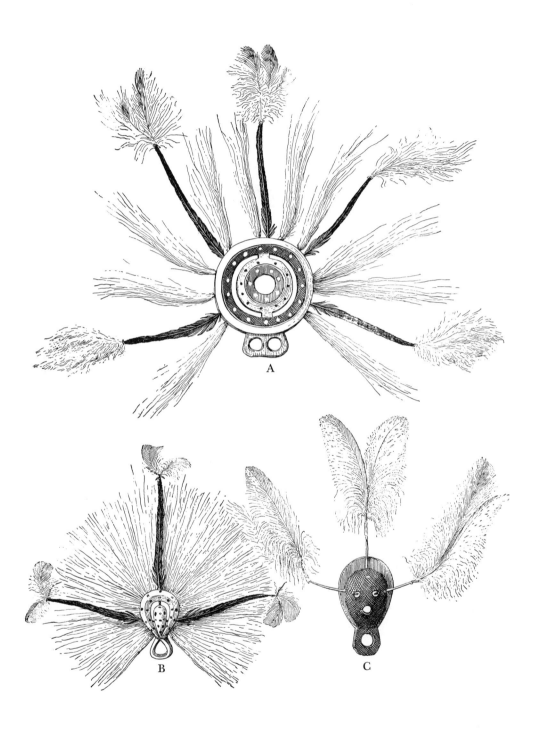

Finger masks used by Eskimo women in their dances. A: From Big Lake. B: From Cape Romanof. C: From Pastolik.

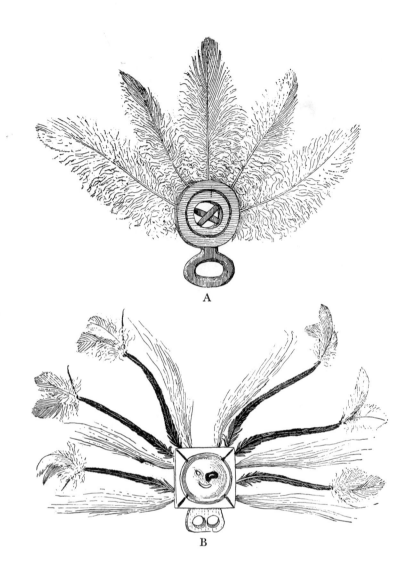

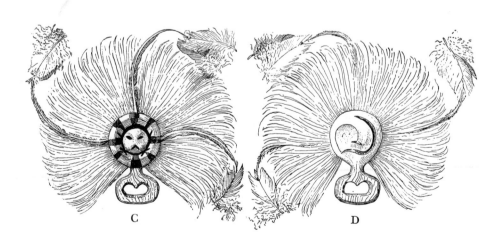

More finger masks used by Eskimo women in their ceremonial dances. A: From Big Lake. B: From Norton Sound. C, D: The rings show how these masks were worn on one or more fingers of the hand.

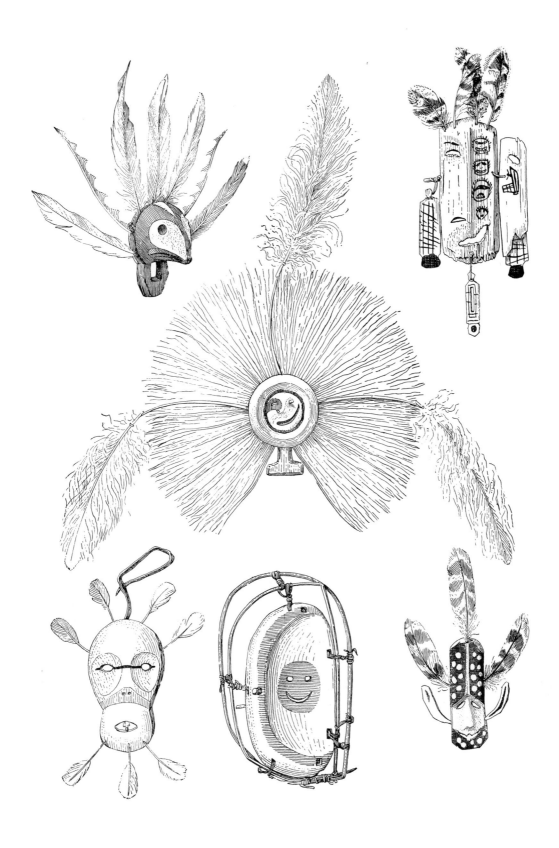

More Eskimos finger masks and "maskoids." Although these pieces are known to have been used in various ceremonials and dances, their exact significance was unknown or forgotten by the end of the nineteenth century, when these examples were collected.

Like the masks on the preceding pages, these masks were used in ceremonials and dances, but their exact significance has been lost. The crude death's head (B) was shaped with fire, as well as carved. The mask D represents the *inua*, or spirit, of the Canada lynx.

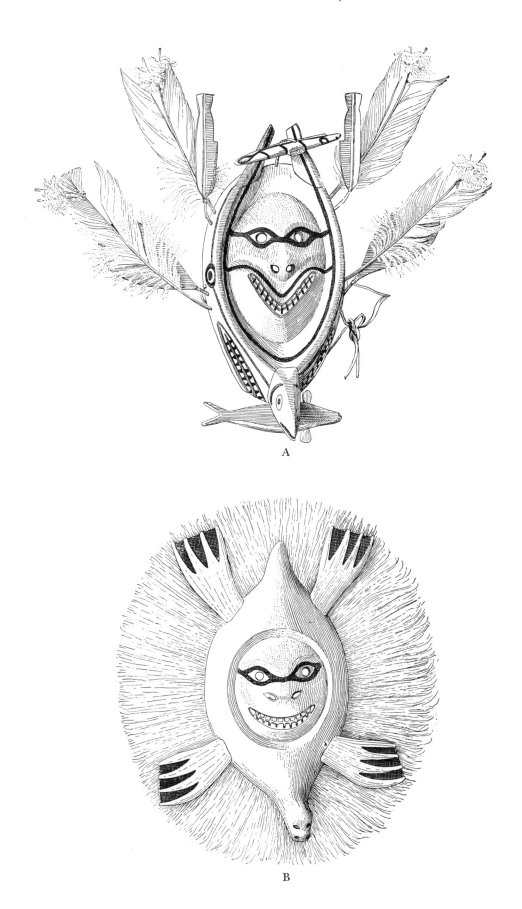

Eskimo masks. A: Salmon from the area south of the Yukon. B: Hair seal. The human faces on these pieces show that they represent the *inua*, or spirit, of the fish or animal.

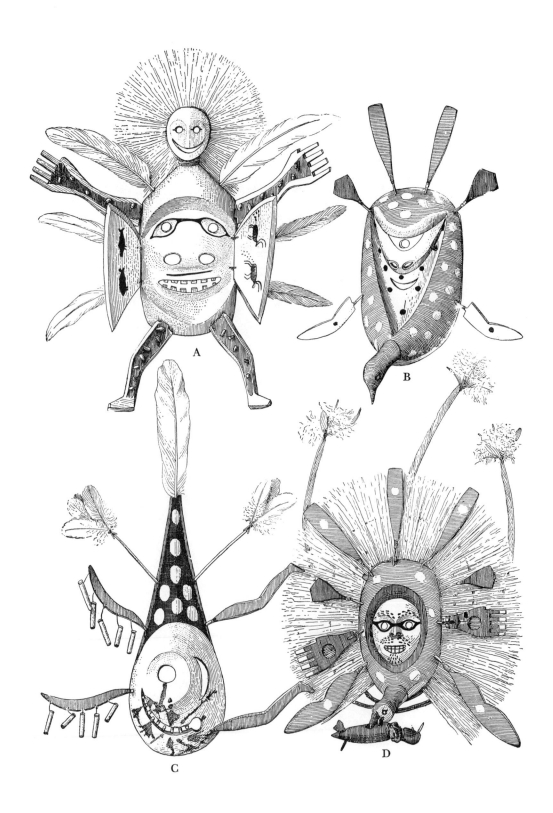

Eskimo masks used in ceremonials. A has movable doors on its face. B represents a guillemot, D a sea parrot (oystercatcher).

Eskimo masks. A represents the *inua* of some species of waterfowl. B, C and D represent
tunghaks, spirits that, according to Eskimo belief, controlled the supply of game.

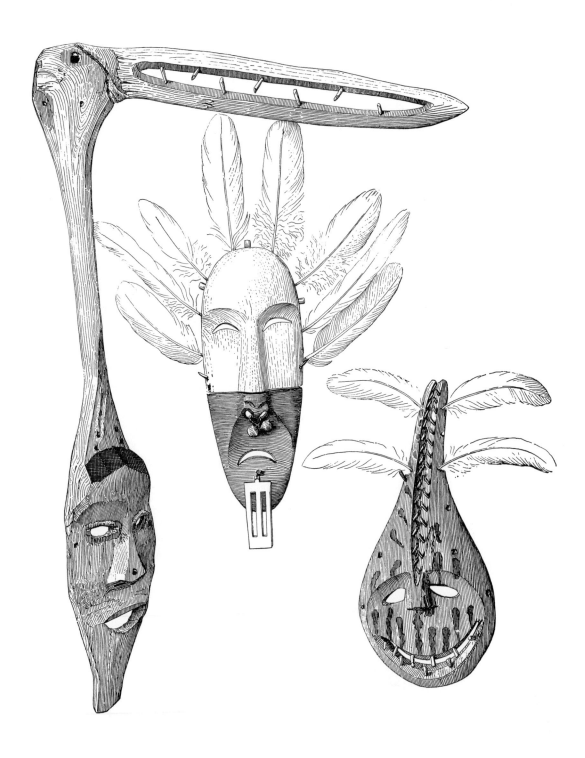

Eskimo masks with grotesque human faces. A is surmounted by the neck and head of a sandhill crane.

Eskimo mask representing a *tunghak*, a being that controlled the supply of game. In this case, the game would appear to be seal, since several figures of seals are attached to the forehead of the mask.

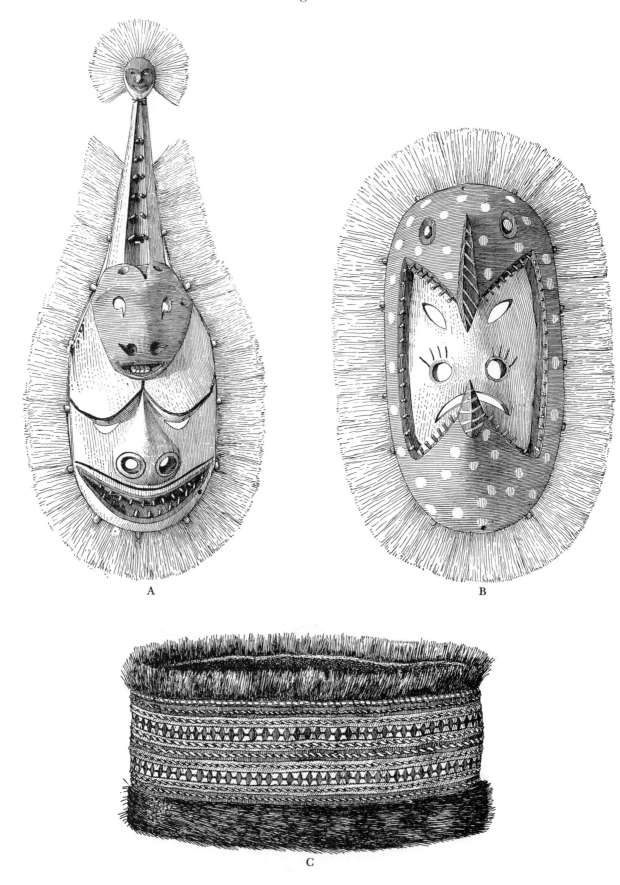

A   B

C

A, B: Masks from Cape Romanof. A has a seal's face above a grotesque semihuman face.
B, carved from a single piece of wood, shows the *inua* (spirit) of a sea parrot enclosed in
the bird's open beak. C: Sealskin wristlet from Ikogmut, used in ceremonial dances.

Eskimo masks. A: The *inua* of a short-eared owl. B: The *inua* of a bear. C: Rare example of a human face without distortion of any kind, representing an Eskimo in a winter hood, with labrets and tattoo marks. D: Semihuman *tunghak*.

Dolls made by Eskimos purely for children's play. Some are carved in ivory, but more are simply and crudely made, at least in comparison with the usual standard of Eskimo carving in the late nineteenth century. The doll in the center wears labrets, has tattoo marks on its upper lip, and is dressed entirely in a traditional fur costume.

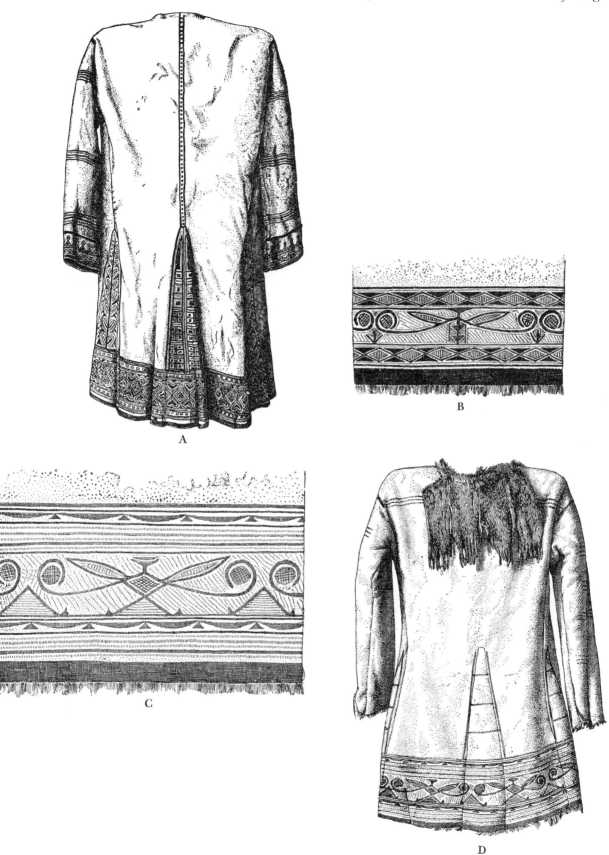

A: Man's buckskin coat with painted decoration, shown from the back. B: Detail of B, page 96; it shows the typical painted decoration often applied to such garments. Startling color combinations were often used in these designs. D: Man's winter coat made by the Hudson's Bay Eskimo, tailored with the hair inside. The skin of the collar is cut in a decorative fringe, and there is a painted border at the hem, a shown in detail in C.

A: Man's winter coat, shown from the front. B, C: Back and front of man's winter coat made from reindeer (caribou) hide by the Ungava Indians in the region of Hudson's Bay. The hood is made separately and then sewn on. The painted border on this coat is shown in detail in B, page 95.

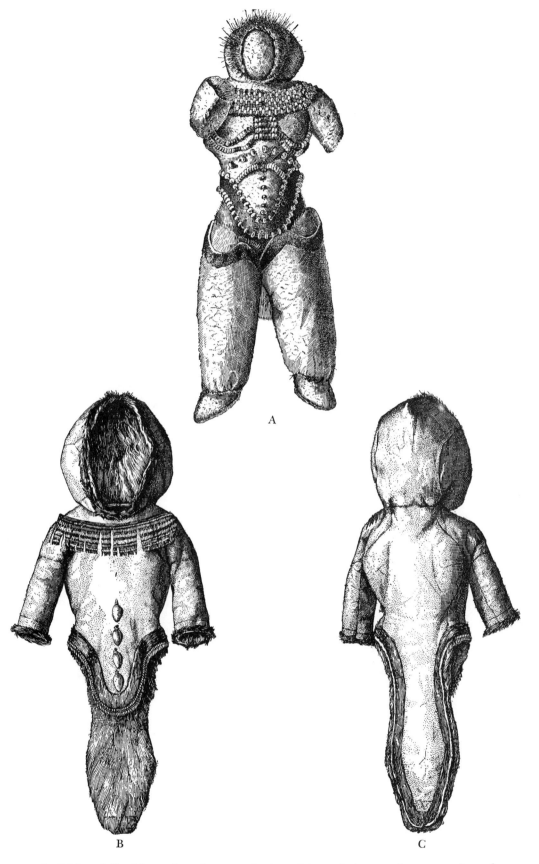

A: Eskimo doll, elaborately and accurately dressed in typical woman's costume, from the area of Hudson's Bay. B, C: Woman's deerskin coat, with back flap for sitting on, and large hood for carrying a baby. The coat is trimmed with pewter spoon bowls down the front while little lead droplets trim the front of the skirt. The collar has a fringe of multi-colored beads.

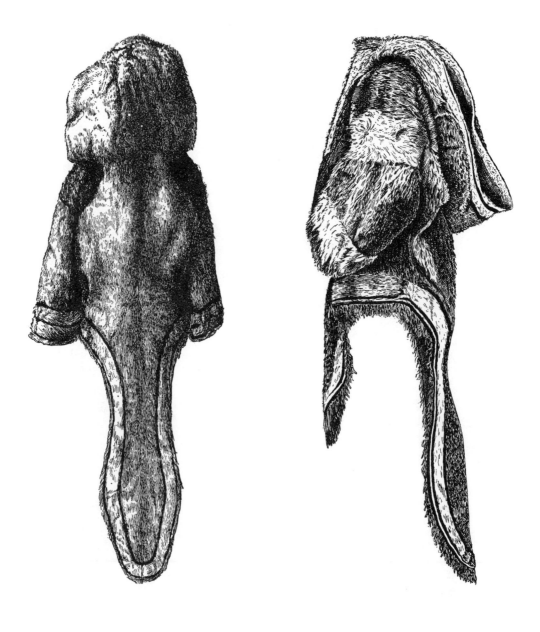

Back and side views of Hudson's Bay Eskimo women's coats, showing the size of the hood and the extent of the front and back flaps on these garments.

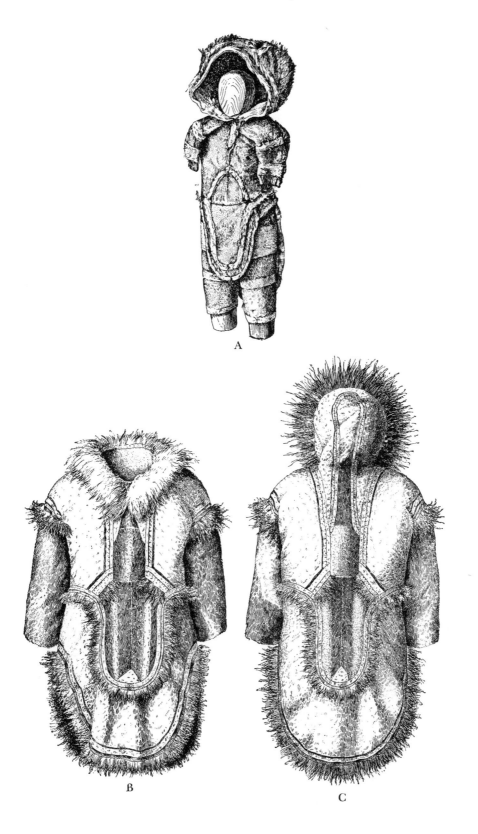

A: Doll dressed in typical Hudson's Bay Eskimo costume. In actual dress, the ends of the leggings would be tucked into high boots. B, C: Unusually handsome Point Barrow (Alaska) Eskimo woman's dress made of shanks and bellies of reindeer pieced together to form light and dark stripes. It is hemmed with white mountain sheep, fawnskin and red worsted (trade cloth), and fringed with wolfskin.

Eskimo drawings of various native and exotic items. A: Bear. B: White trader. C: European sailing ship. E: Caribou. F, G: Eskimo women.

Eskimo drawings from Alaska, including several figures of women, and a hunting scene.

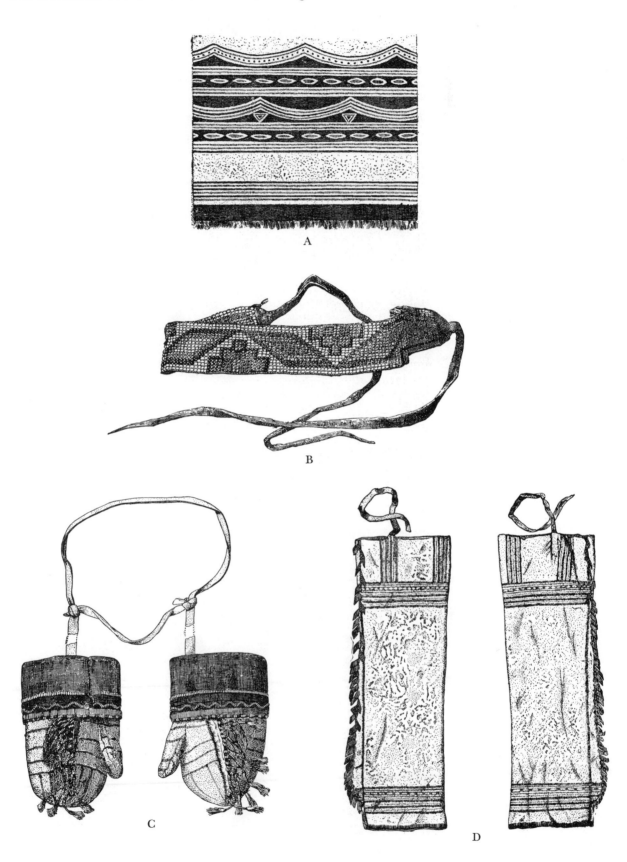

Clothing and decorations from the Hudson's Bay region. A: Pattern painted on a deerskin robe. B: Beaded headband from the Nenenot tribe, often made by the women for their husbands or lovers. C: Mittens made of smoked deerskin, lined with unborn reindeer fur. D: Leather leg coverings for the upper part of legs, made in the two distinct pieces characteristic of Indian dress of this area.

A

B

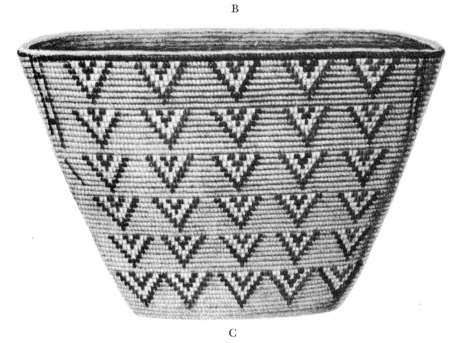

C

Northwest Coast basketry. A: Small Tlingit basket with a design representing a mountain called Tsalxan. B: Lillooet basket with a design in beading. C: Thompson basket with a design variously called "butterfly," "butterfly cut off," "butterfly wings" and "arrowhead."

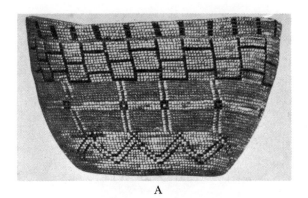

A

B

C

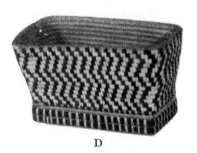

D

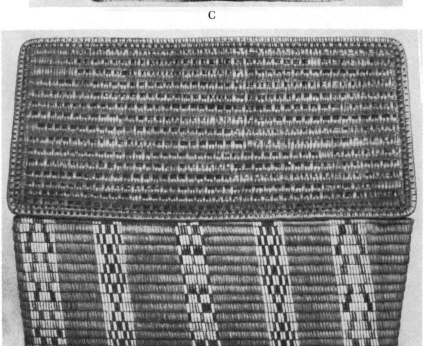

E

F

British Columbia baskets. A: Chilcotin basket with a number of different designs. B: Thompson tobacco basket with lid, with a design known as "snake" or "garter snake." C: Thompson basket with "mouth" or "notch" design that some say was adapted from the whites. D: Utamqt basket with vertical zigzag design. E: Lillooet basket with vertical stripe designs: rows 1 and 5 are "arrowhead" design, 2 and 4 "Indian rice" design, and the center "snake" or "fly." F: Chilcotin basket with watchspring-coiling on lid.

A: Thompson basket with fret design. B: Thompson basket with diamond design. C: Lillooet basket with two-field arrangement and a realistic design of quadrupeds. D: Chilcotin basket with vertical zigzag and stepped fret design. E: Thompson basket with vertical striped design. F: Utamqt basket with diamond design.

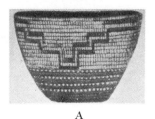

A

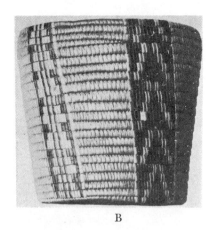

B

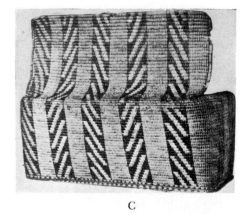

C

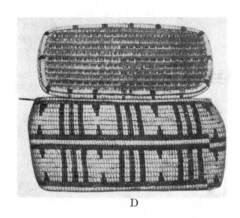

D

E

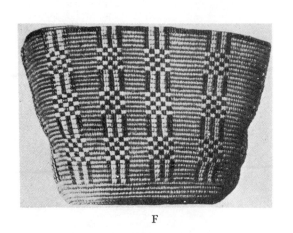

F

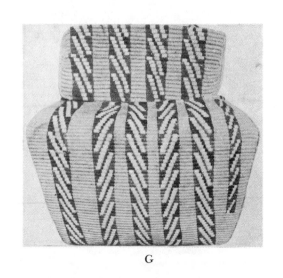

G

A: Lillooet basket with beading on lower field of design. B: Lillooet basket with vertical stripes and chevron design. C: Thompson basket (probably), with lid and a vertical stripe design of bars, or "half-arrowheads." D: Lillooet basket with lid, and design of "scratches," "short points," "teeth" or "incisions." E: Thompson basket with "hook," "angle," "single crook," "duck" or "duck's head" pattern. F: Thompson basket with "necklace of bead" and "dentalia" pattern. G: Thompson basket with vertical stripes of "half-arrowheads," "arrowpoint" or "dentalia" design.

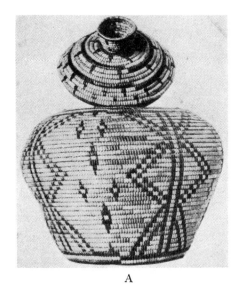

A

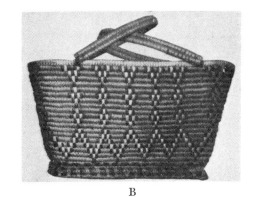

B

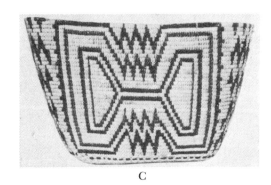

C

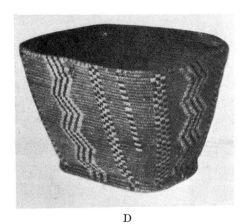

D

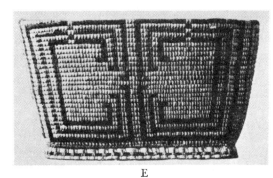

E

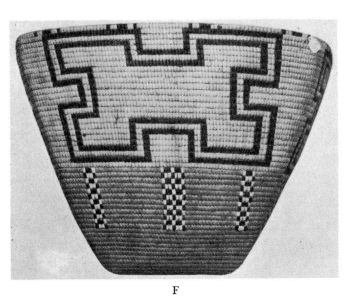

F

G

A: Lillooet basket with "arrowhead" and a variety of ladder design. B: Lower Thompson basket with diamond and zigzag design. C: Thompson basket with mixed "butterfly" and "leaves" design. D: Thompson basket with vertical stripes of "snake," "pack-strap" and "fly" designs. E: Thompson basket with incomplete rectangular enclosures. F: Lillooet basket with a variety of "mouth" design. G: Lillooet basket with design called "intestines" by that tribe.

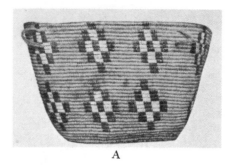

A

B

C

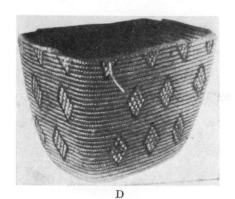

D

E

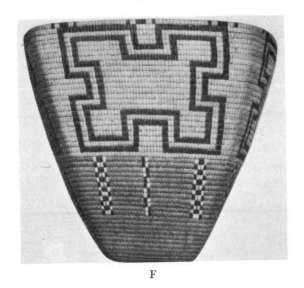

F

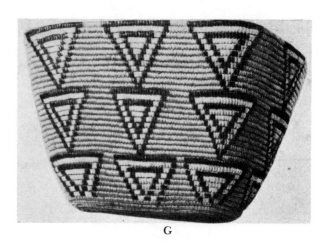

G

A: Thompson basket with design of "stars." B: Thompson basket with "arrowheads," "arrowpoints," "deer fence with snares" or zigzag designs. C: Thompson basket with zigzag stripes. D: Thompson basket with a design of "Indian rice." E: Thompson basket with "cross" or "star" design. F: Lillooet basket with "intestine" design, called by Thompson Indians "caterpillar design made in a circle." G: Thompson basket with vertical arrangement of a triangular design.

A

B

C

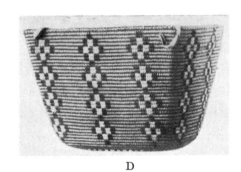

D

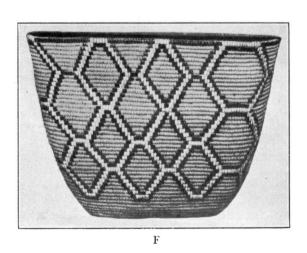

F

E

G

A: Thompson basket with large single design. B: Thompson basket with sharply pointed zigzags or "arrowpoints." C: Lillooet ladder design with naturalistic motifs. D: Thompson basket with a vertical arrangement of the "star" design. E: Thompson basket with "notch," "mouth" or variations of "grave-box." F: Thompson basket with "fish net," or as it is sometimes called, "deer net" design. G: Thompson basket with designs of "necklace of dentalia and beads," "rattlesnake tail" and "flying goose."

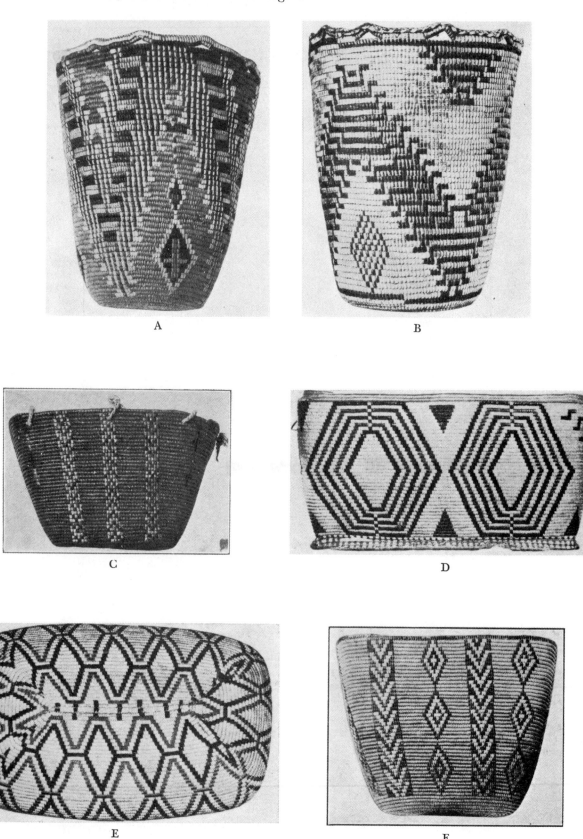

A, B: Klickitat baskets with the zigzag designs common in that tribe's basketry. C: Thompson basket with "snake," "bead" or "embroidery" design. D: Thompson basket with hexagonal design. E: Thompson basket with "fish net" (or "deer net") design. F: Thompson basket with bands of "arrowheads," or "leaves," and "lakes," or "eyes."

A – K

L   M

N

A–M: Thompson baskets in a variety of shapes and designs, from strictly geometrical to naturalistic subjects. L: "Snake" or "snakeskin" design. N: Lillooet basket with a "white man's design," copied from the border of a handkerchief.

A

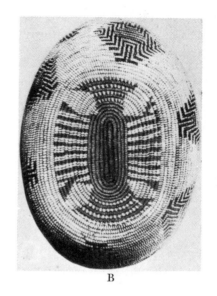

B

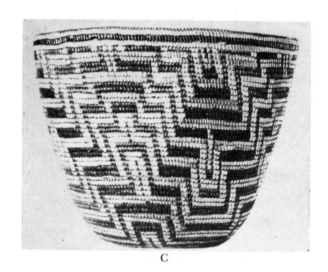

C

D

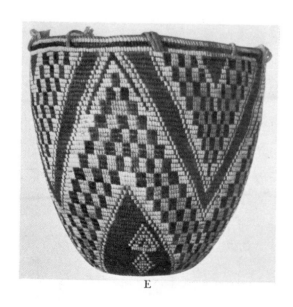

E

F

Klickitat baskets with typical zigzag designs arranged horizontally, often covering the entire field of the basket. The design of F, with its elaboration of simple elements, was called a "false" design by the Klickitats.

A

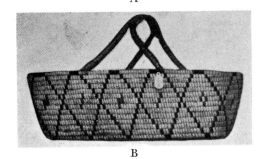

B

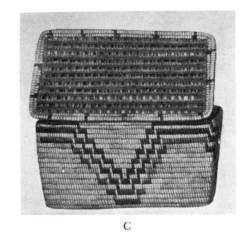

C

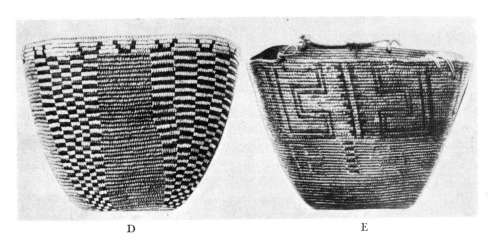

D   E

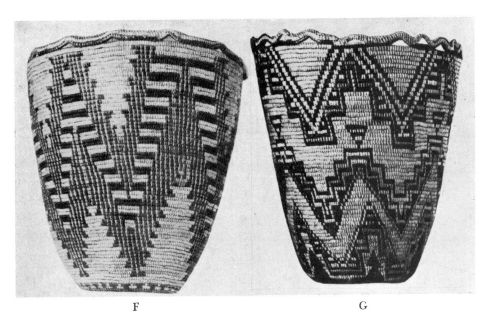

F   G

A: Lillooet basket with design called "snake track" or "necklace." B: Lillooet basket with "net" design. C: Lillooet basket with "necklace" design. D: Thompson basket with geòmetrical design. E: Lillooet basket with "notched" design. F, G: Klickitat baskets with zigzag designs arranged horizontally in patterns typical of the basketry of this tribe.

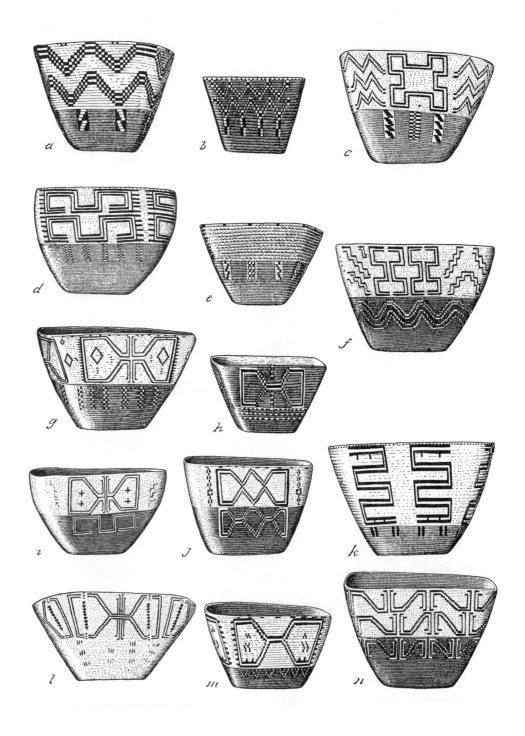

Lillooet baskets. G–N are decorated with "butterfly" or modified "butterfly" designs. Others have zigzag or vertical stripe designs. F has an abstract design at the top called "hand hammers," with a "mountain" pattern at the bottom.

Klickitat woven bags using some of the same designs employed in basketry: "net" and zig-zag designs in horizontal arrangements.

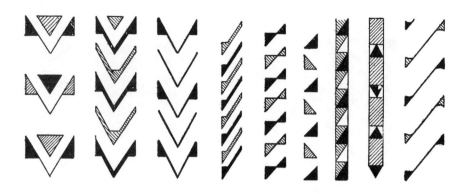

A: Abstract basket designs from Lytton, including "flying bird," designs used vertically. B: Realistic motifs used in British Columbian basketry: tipis, lodges, arrows and so forth. While the origin of some of the designs is obvious, others are inexplicable, and all traces of derivation have been lost.

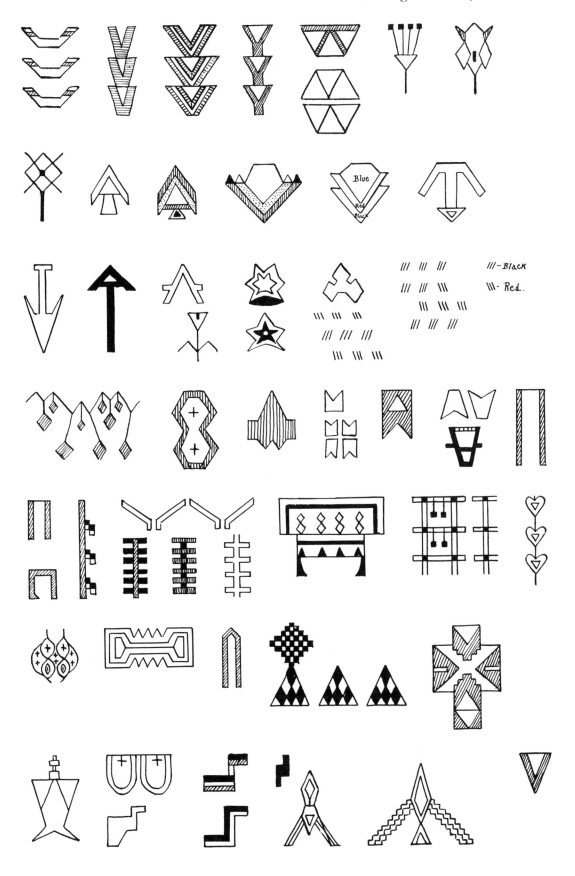

Designs used in British Columbian basketry, including realistic, geometric and strongly conventionalized designs.

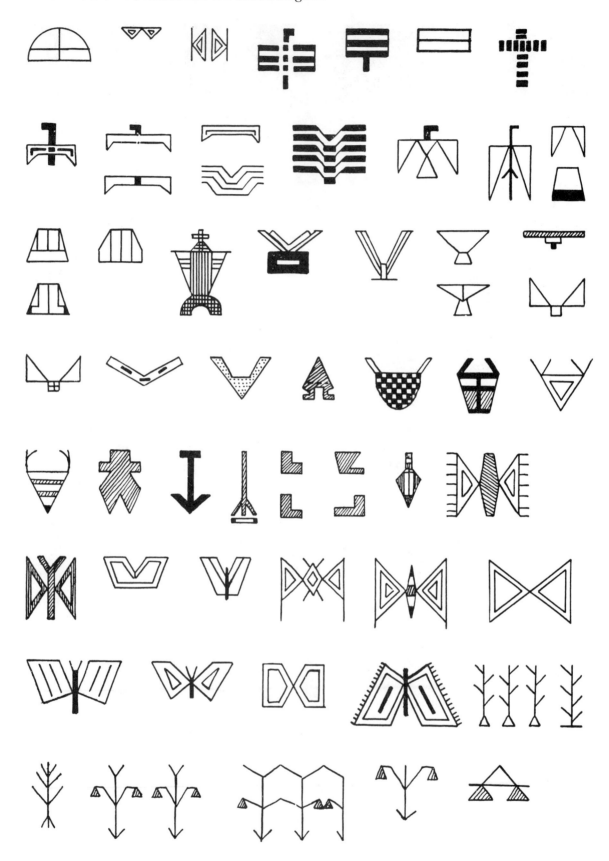

Strongly conventionalized designs based on realistic objects: sweat house, butterfly, eagle and other birds, and trees.

Elements of various geometric designs: diamonds, rhomboids, trapezoids, hexagons, octagons and combinations of various simple geometric figures.

Simple geometric figures and combinations, as well as various geometric and realistic designs. Combinations of these designs often form such familiar patterns in basketry as "star," "arrowhead" and "leaf." Realistic motifs include "snake," "lizard," "hand" and "butterfly."

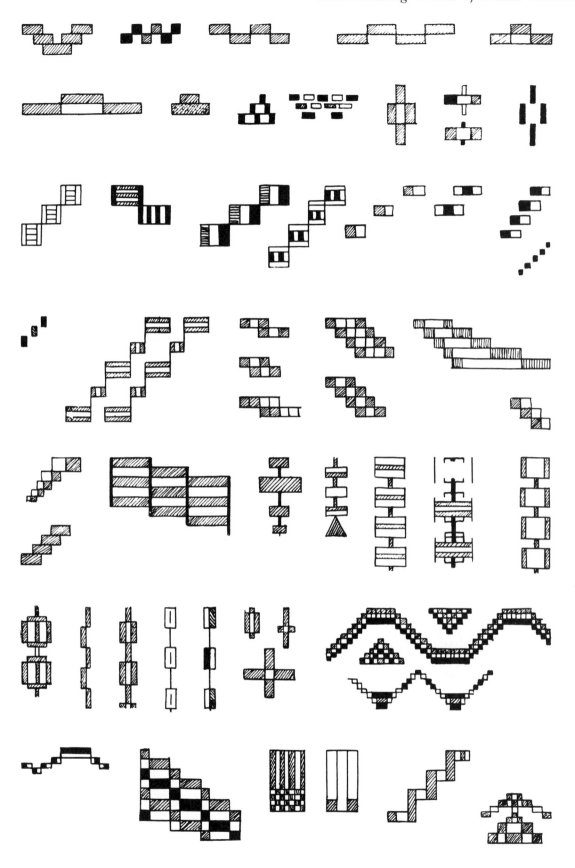

Designs derived from combinations of rectangles arranged horizontally, vertically and in ladders. Various traditional names are given for each design: "cross," "star," "morning star" and so forth.

Designs based on rectangles and diamonds. Traditional names such as "spearhead," "arrowhead," "contracting eye" and "net" are often applied to such designs.

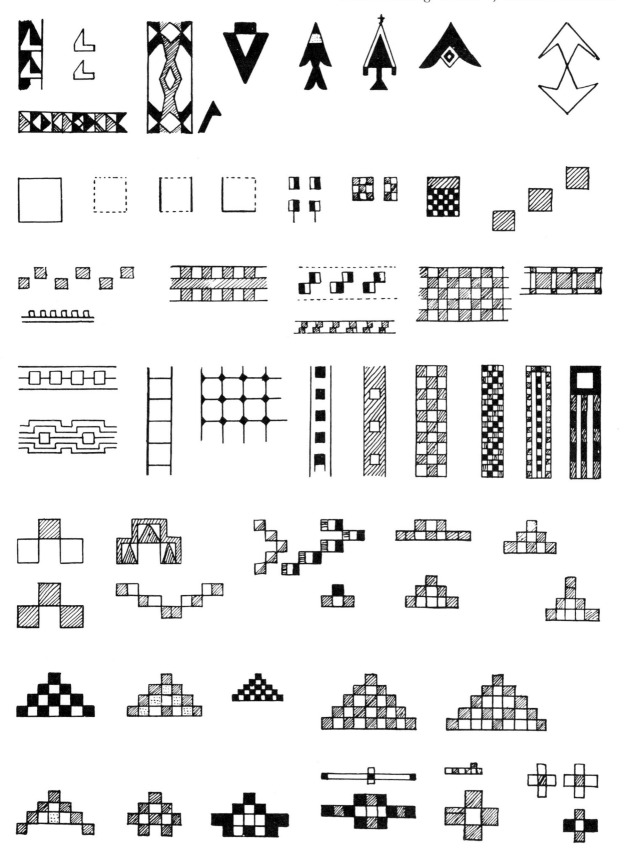

Designs based on triangles and squares, some with various traditional names such as "arrowhead," "bird," "deer net," "caterpillar" and "embroidery."

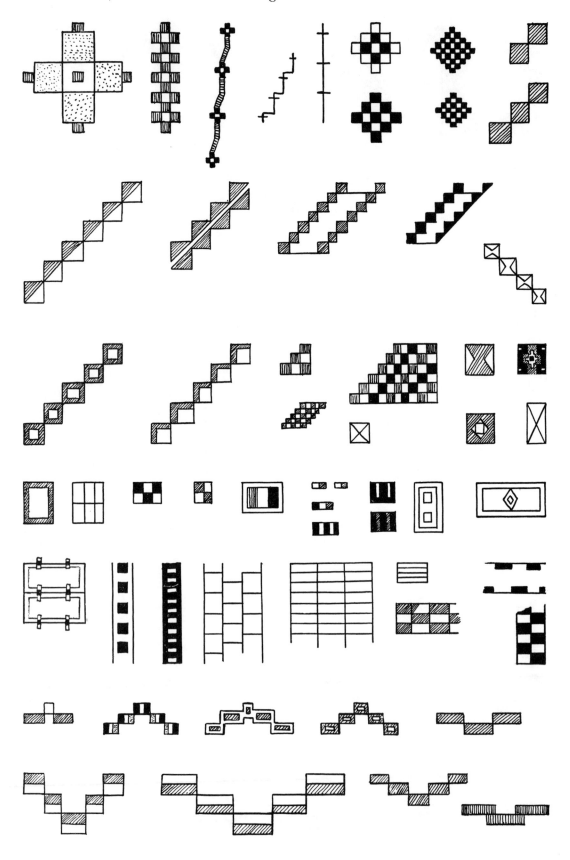

Designs made of combinations of squares and rectangles. Traditional names for these patterns include "ladder," "arrowhead," "star," "hairy caterpillar," "snakeskin," "butterfly" and "flying goose."

Designs featuring meanders, crossed lines and triangles. Names for these designs include
"clouds," "mountains," "star," "arrowhead," "leaf" and "butterfly."

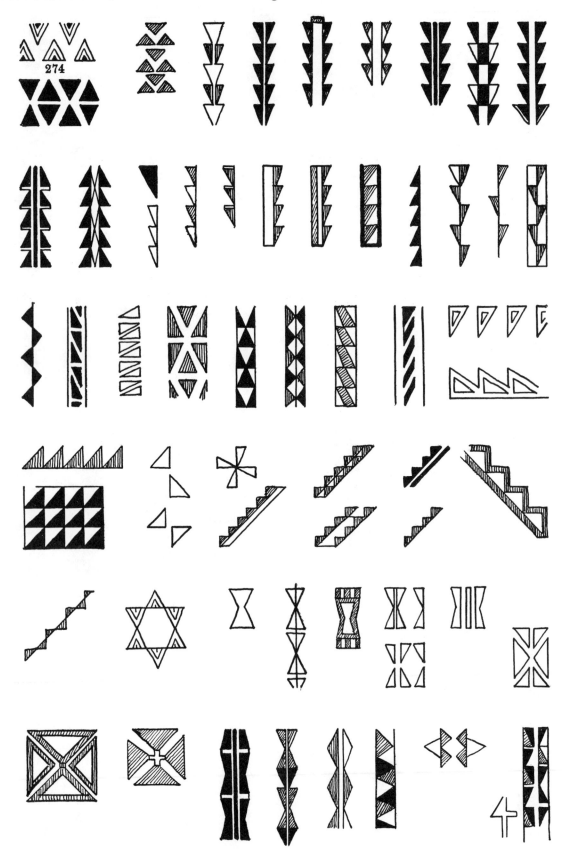

Designs based on combinations of triangles. The most common names for these designs
are "arrowhead" or "ladder" design; occasionally they are called "leaf" or "caterpillar."

Designs derived from diagonal zigzags in vertical arrangements. Zigzags composed of horizontal and vertical sections are known as "snake," "caterpillar" and "snake track." Chevron designs are frequently known as "butterfly wing," "arrowpoint" or "fish backbone."

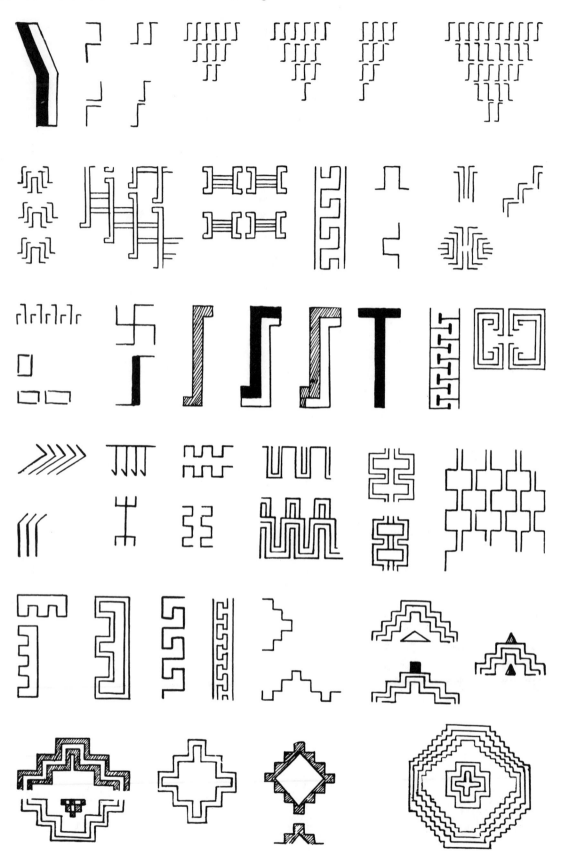

Designs composed of chevrons, right angles and meanders. Chevron designs are frequently called "rainbow." Those with right angles are known as "grasshopper," "caterpillar," "bent leg" or "foot." Meander designs have various names, such as "snakes," "notches," "grave-boxes," "clouds" or "mountains."

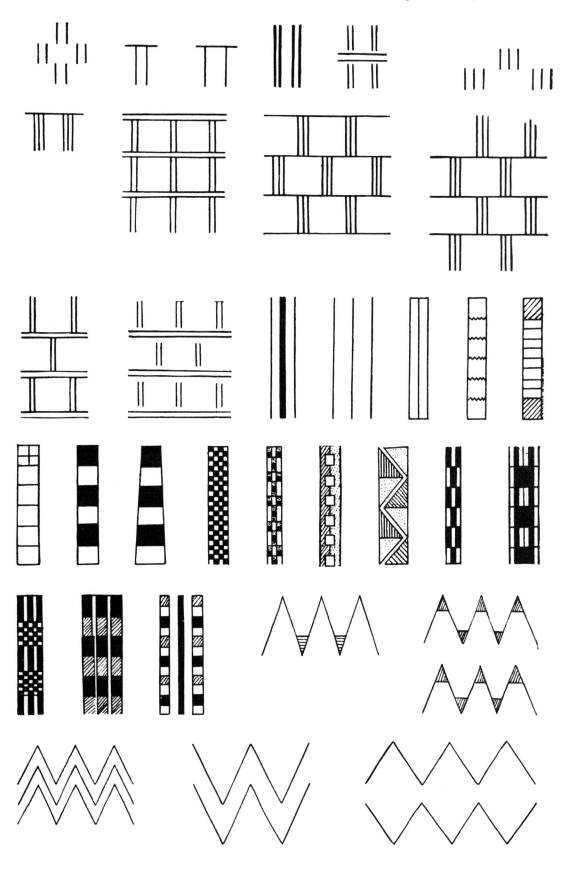

Designs composed of combinations of vertical, diagonal, zigzag and horizontal lines.

Designs based on diagonals, zigzags, and horizontal and vertical arrangements of lines.
Traditional names for these designs include "snake track," "grasshopper," "wave," "necklace," "embroidery" and "arrowpoint."

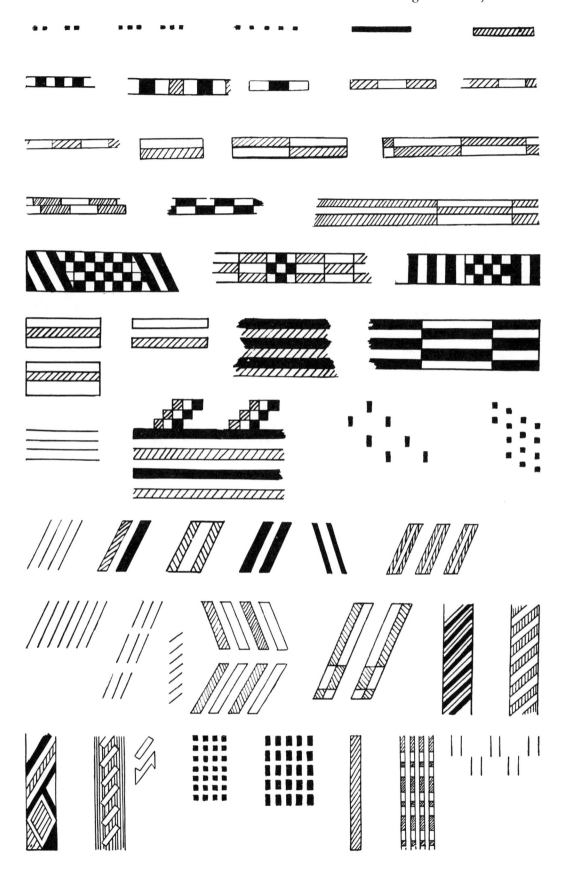

Combinations of horizontal, diagonal and vertical lines, from simple "spot" designs to complex borders.

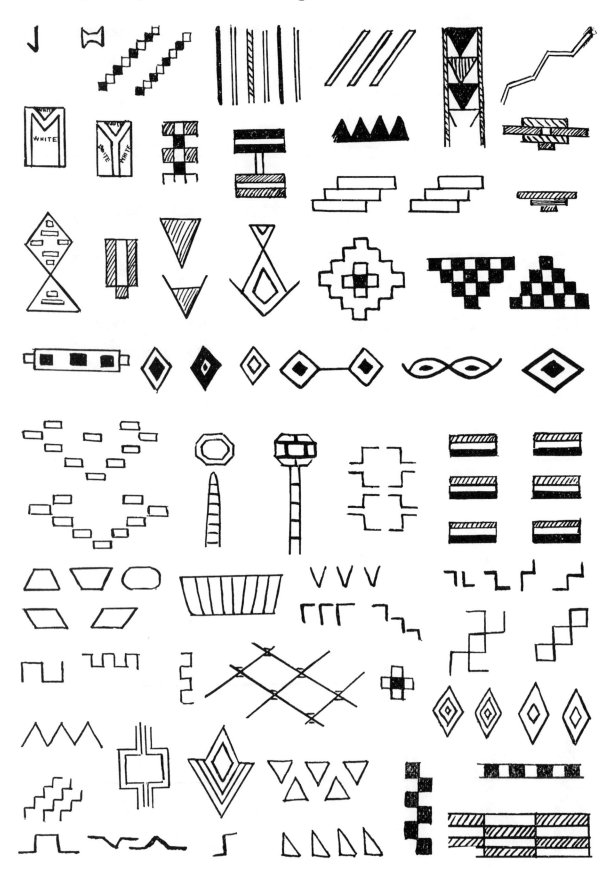

Designs made by individual artists of the upper Thompson tribe, showing how simple geometric designs of diamonds, squares, rectangles and triangles were built up into frets and meanders.

Late nineteenth-century basket designs, described as innovations by the Thompson Indians in the 1890s. Most of these were either borrowed from the whites or from the Plains tribes, or resulted from new combinations of traditional elements.

Rows A–D: Late nineteenth-century basket designs of the Thompson Indians, mostly geometric, based on diamonds arranged in horizontal and vertical bands. E–K: Older Thompson basket designs, showing a variety of geometrical elements. Some of these patterns were already obsolete at the time the baskets were collected.

Rows A–G: "Embroidery" designs from Thompson baskets, developed from quillwork and embroidery on clothing. H–M: Basket designs gathered among the Thompson Indians which the Indians themselves considered "old" at the time (1890s). They consist mostly of outline designs, some obsolete, some still in use at the time of collecting.

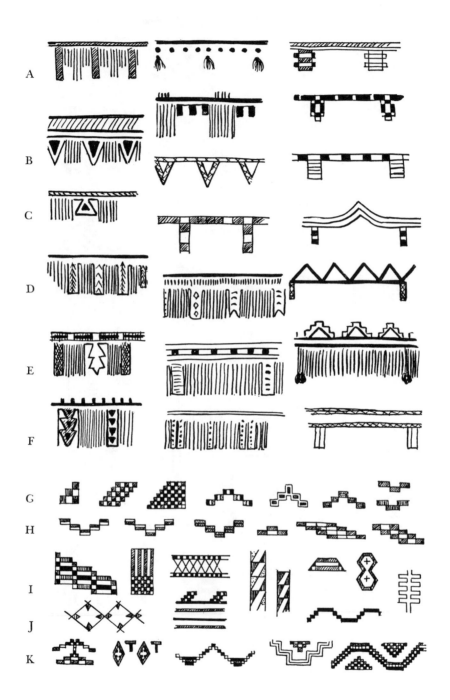

Rows A–F: Fringes used as decoration on clothing and other items by various tribes, thought to have had an influence on basketry design. G–K: "Embroidery" designs on Thompson baskets, derived from quillwork and embroidery on clothing.

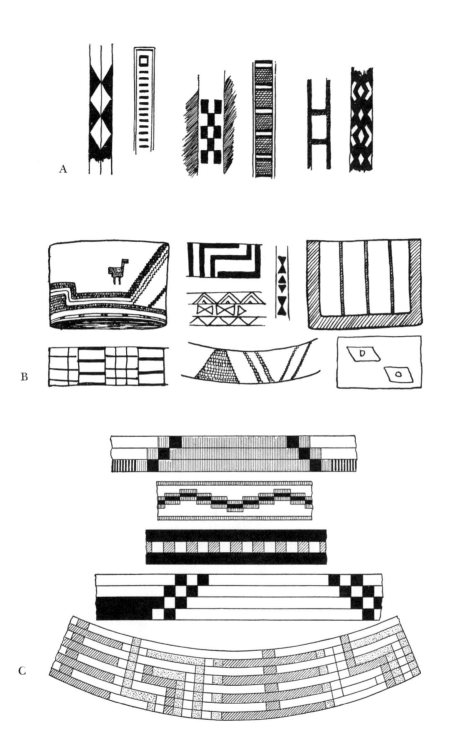

A: Beading designs used on baskets in vertical stripes. B: Quillwork from Alaska on a Tlingit basket. C: Quillwork and basket embroidery patterns from Alaska. Quillwork patterns were later adapted to basketry decoration.

Chilcotin designs based on various single relements, such as zigzags, diamonds, triangles, stepped designs and so on. Although geometric in form, they often have various realistic interpretations, such as "arrowhead."

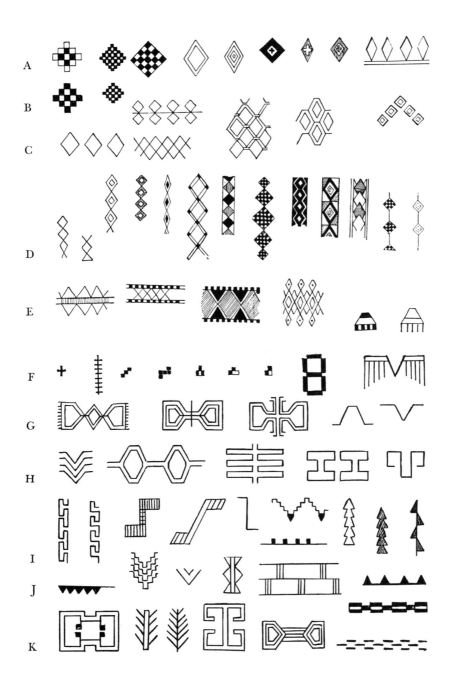

Rows A–E: Various designs based on triangles and trapezoids. Trapezoidal designs are rare and are often called "moss cake," "teeth" or "butterfly wings." F–K: Lillooet designs, including various "fly" designs or "spots," some arranged in vertical or horizontal series.

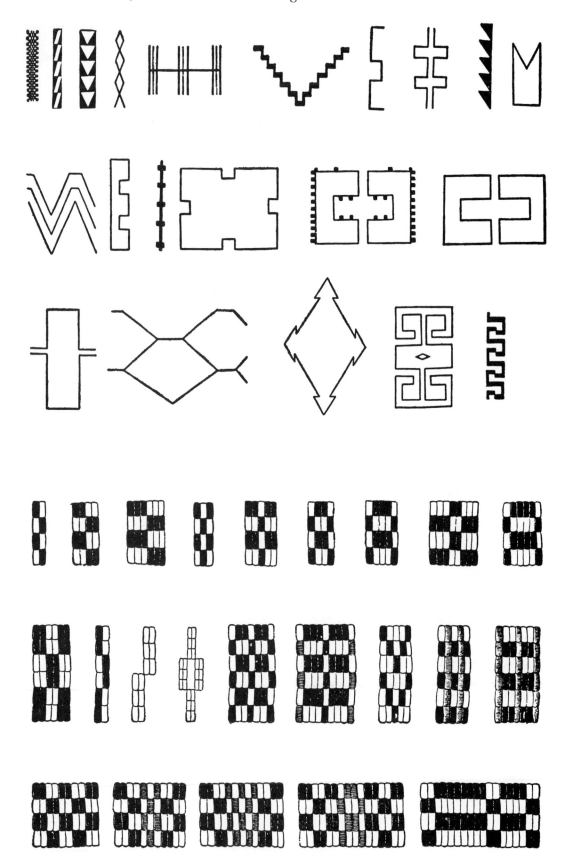

Lillooet designs, such as "fly," "arrowhead," "net" and "ladder," along with various "fly" patterns in vertical and horizontal bands.

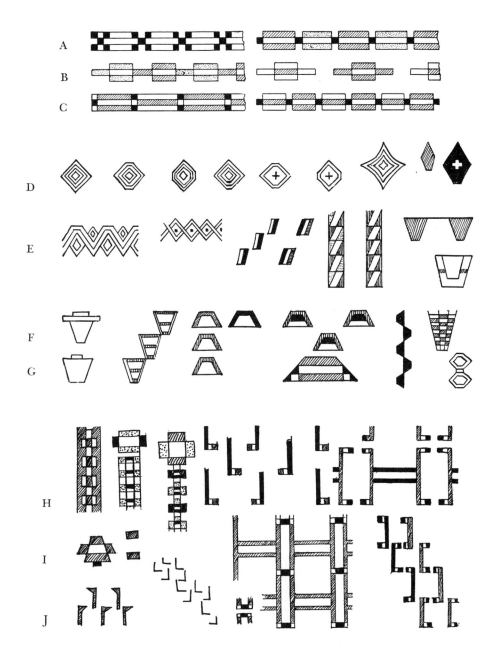

Rows A–C: Basket designs from Lytton, with "chain" and "notch" or "necklace." These served as embroidery as well as basketry designs. D–G: Basket designs featuring more trapezoidal and rhomboidal designs. Rhomboidal figures are usually found as elements in connected designs often called "dentalia" or "embroidery." H–J: Basket designs from Lytton, called "stars" when large, "flies" when small. Others are variations of the "leg" design, whose original meaning is now lost. "Leg" designs can be joined in connected patterns or broken and scattered over a field.

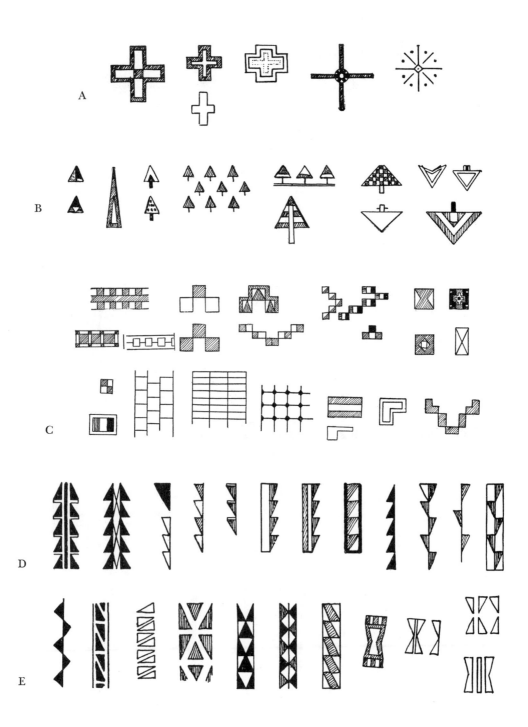

Designs derived from rectangles, squares, triangles and zigzags in various combinations. A: Motifs usually known as "stars," sometimes as "flying birds" or "flies." Despite their shape, these motifs have no connection with the Christian cross. B: Triangular designs usually called "arrowheads"; a second group is designated as "trees," "shrubs" or occasionally "mushrooms." C: Checkered designs interpreted by various tribes in the aggregate as "clusters of flies," or "clusters of stars," or "Indian-rice root" or "cloud." D, E: Ladder designs, composed of triangles, thus called from their resemblance to the notched logs used as ladders. The name is used even when the design is applied horizontally. Such triangular patterns may have come from Plains Indian art.

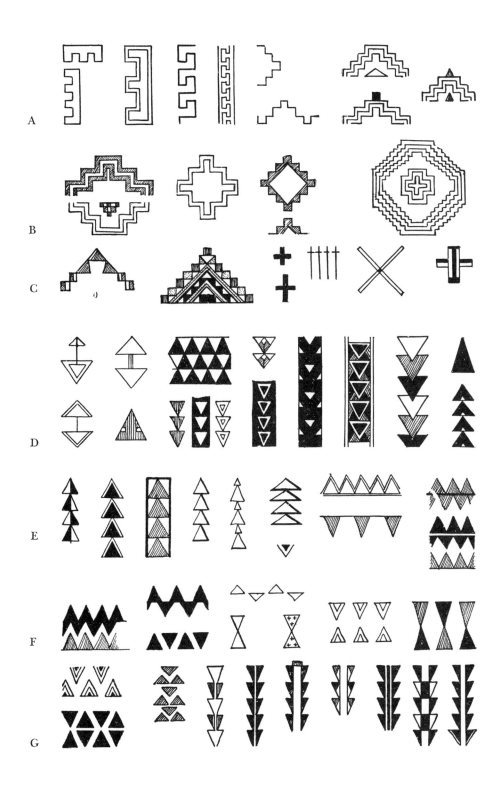

A: Designs based on meanders, generally called "mouth" or "notch," whether arranged horizontally or vertically. More elaborate meanders, such as the one at the right, are called "zigzags," "steps," "mountains," "clouds" and "necklaces." B: "Notched" or "stepped stars." Row C includes interpretations of the Christian cross. D–G: Ladder designs based on triangles arranged horizontally and vertically.

Designs based on zigzags, often called "snake track," "worm" or "lightning." The pyramidal zigzag is sometimes called "mountain" or "necklace." A chevron pointing downward was called "arrowpoint," "angle" or "butterfly wing." In vertical arrangements, it was called "arrowpoint" only. Chevrons connected with vertical lines through the points became "trees" or "branches." With a horizontal line, they were known as "wave," "angle," "zigzag," "bent leg" or "ribs." Triangles and zigzags were known as "mountains," "clouds," "necklace," "pendants" and "arrowpoints."

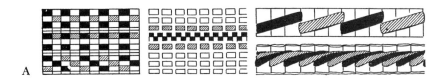

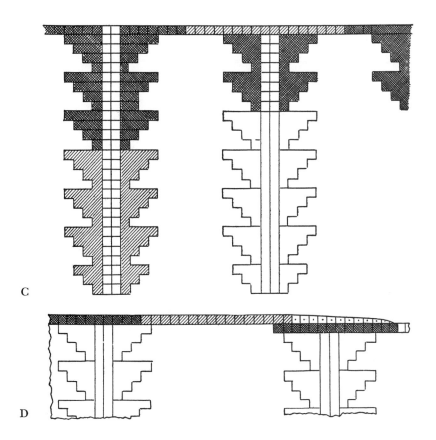

A: Methods of beading. B: Beaded designs for baby carriers. C, D: Stepped triangles arranged in vertical stripes.

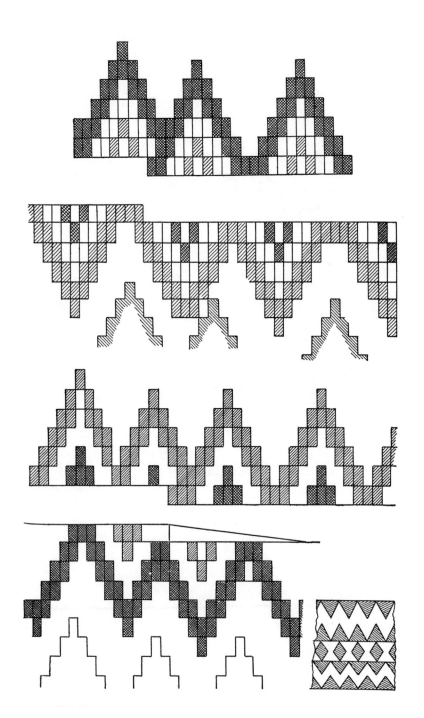

A group of zigzag patterns forming stepped triangles. Arranged horizontally, they show the adjustment of the pattern to the sides of the basket.

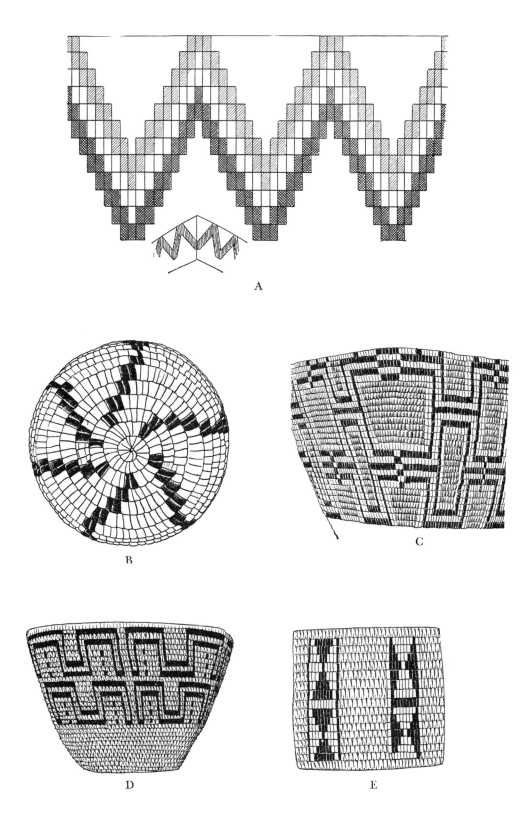

A: Zigzag pattern used on a basket. B: Lid design for basket. C: Basket with meander design covering the entire field. D: Meander, "notch," or "mouth" design on basket. E: Triangular patterns arranged in vertical stripes.

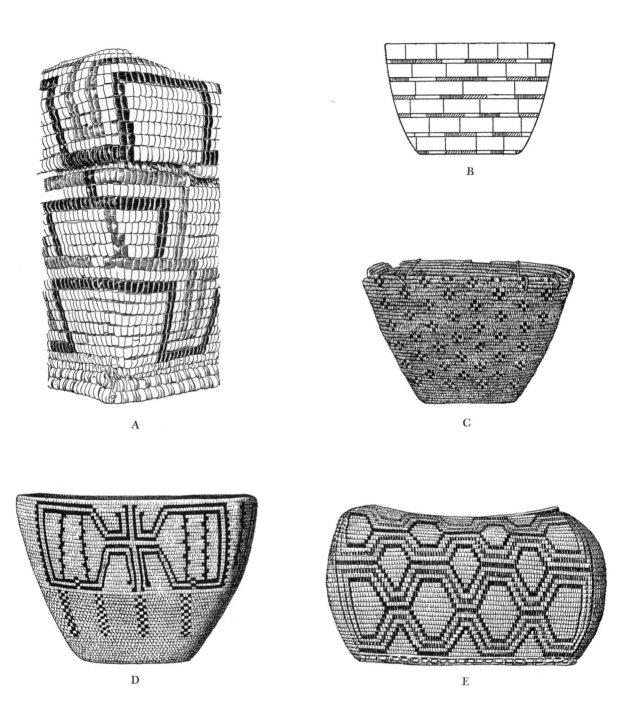

A: Corner of basket showing adaptation of meander or "notched" design. B: Banded decoration on basket. C: Basket with allover "star" design. D: Lillooet basket with "butterfly" design and beaded stripes. E: Lillooet basket with allover design sometimes known as "grave-box."

THE SOUTHWEST

Ancient Pueblo pottery. A–C: Food bowls from Pueblo Viejo in the upper Gila Valley, Arizona, showing continuous external decoration of zigzags, meanders and terraced forms. D: Vase from Pueblo Viejo, with continuous external decoration of various geometric forms, including spirals and meanders.

Ancient Pueblo pottery. A: Food bowl from Shumopovi, with exterior decoration of continuous geometric designs. B: Pitcher from Four-Mile Ruin, Arizona, combining geometrical decoration with a conventionalized bird design. C: Vase from Chevlon, Arizona, in red,
black and white ware, bearing continuous geometrical decoration both internally and ex-
ternally.

Ancient Pueblo pottery. A: Vase from Four-Mile Ruin, Arizona, with typical continuous designs, bands and meanders. B: Vase from Four-Mile Ruin, with geometric design of bands and dots. C: Vase from Chevlon Ruin with design of meanders, zigzags and bands.

Ancient Pueblo pottery. A: Tusayan vase of eccentric form. B: Handled cup from the area of Cibola. C: Vase from Homolobi with four bird figures. D: Vase from eastern Arizona, showing neck and body decoration with meanders in two sizes, and applied decoration of a small animal head. E: Handled mug from the area of Tusayan. F: Vase with decoration in dark paint on white ground from the area of Tusayan.

Ancient Pueblo pottery. A: Figure of an animal's paw (perhaps a bear or badger) found on the bottom of a vase. B: Bowl from Kanab, Utah, with design on the interior. C: Exterior decoration on the bowl in which the animal's paw (A) was found. D: Globular vase, ornamented with bands of meanders, from the area of Tusayan. E: Vase of eccentric form from eastern Arizona. F: Handled vase from the area of Tusayan.

Ancient Pueblo pottery. A: Food vessel from Four-Mile Ruin, Arizona, with conventional-
ized animal design, perhaps a lizard, horned toad or even a raccoon. B: Food bowl from
Chevlon with interior geometrical decoration. C: Vase from Pueblo Viejo in the upper
Gila Valley, Arizona, showing decoration around the neck.

Ancient Pueblo pottery. A, B: Food bowls from Epley's Ruin, Gila Valley, Arizona, with interior decoration of (A) terraced designs, diamonds and dots, and (B) zigzags. C: Food bowl from Shumopovi, Arizona, decorated with a human head, probably a masked figure of a dancer. The left eye resembles the eye treatment in certain Zuñi masks.

Ancient Pueblo pottery. A: Food bowl from Shumopovi with interior decoration of a plumed snake (?). B: Food bowl from Chevlon, with continuous internal and external decoration in red, black and white in geometric patterns. C: Food bowl from Chevlon. The interior decoration features a quadruped identified by the Hopi as a buffalo. The beast has a hump, but no horns.

Ancient Pueblo pottery. A: Food bowl from Homolobi, Arizona, with geometrical designs. B: Food bowl from Shumopovi with a bird design on the interior. The canes that form part of the design were used in a gambling game until at least the end of the nineteenth century. C: Food bowl from Four-Mile Ruin with a unique design of unknown meaning.

Ancient Pueblo pottery. A: Painting design on the interior of a food bowl, consisting of meanders and zigzags. B: Food bowl with a sun emblem from Four-Mile Ruin. The radiating bars may also indicate feathers. C: Food bowl with bird design from Four-Mile Ruin. An unusual feature is the teeth on the beak, indicating a mythic rather than a natural bird. D: Painted design on the interior of a food bowl, with meanders, zigzags, scrolls and circles. The area of the bowl is divided into two fields, and each field is quartered.

Ancient Pueblo pottery. A: Painted design from the interior of a food bowl, with stripes and meanders arranged in a swirled pattern. B: Food bowl from Four-Mile Ruin with a cloud pattern, symbol of the rainbow. C: Food bowl from Four-Mile Ruin with a human figure, apparently wearing a mask with a crest of feathers like a Hopi shalako (katcina), indicating that the culture that made the pottery was familiar with katcinas. D: Interior of a food bowl with bands of meanders used in a swirling design.

Ancient Pueblo pottery. A: Plumed-serpent motif from the interior of a food basin from Sikyatki. B: Unidentified reptile, highly conventionalized, from the interior of a Sikyatki food bowl. It appears to be a combination of bird and reptile with tail feathers and wings. C: Another animal in highly conventionalized form, combining reptilian and avian features. D: Bird-man, probably a mythological personage. It appears to be wearing a feathered headdress.

Ancient Pueblo pottery. Figures of birds, some very greatly conventionalized, from the interiors of food bowls found at the ruins of Sikyatki.

Ancient Pueblo pottery. A: Decoration with human figures from the interior of a food bowl excavated from a mound at St. George, Utah. B: Food bowl with geometrical design from Chaves Pass, with spiral figures and S-shaped ornaments on the bands. C: Food bowl from Homolobi, with an interior decoration of a spider and sun emblem (Spider was the mother of the twin war-gods of the Hopi). D: Painted device on the interior of a food bowl from Kanab, Utah.

A

B

C

D

Ancient Pueblo pottery. A: Painted meander design from a handled bowl from the area of Tusayan. B: Bird figure on a bowl from Chevlon. The features are reptilian rather than avian. Particularly unusual is the treatment of the tail. C: Bowl from Chevlon with "three lines of life," a traditional name for the encircling broken bands. A terraced design is here built up into a complex pattern. D: Interior design of continuous meanders from a piece of pottery excavated from the tumulus at St. George, Utah.

A

B

C

D

Ancient Pueblo pottery. A: Design from the interior of a food bowl. Because the scroll ornament was crowded into a circular shape and distorted, the center is left with a space shaped like a four-pointed star. B: Bird figure on a food bowl from Chevlon, with unusual tail and teeth. C: Interior of a vessel from Chevlon with a rain-cloud figure and birds. D: Interior decoration on a food bowl from the area of Tusayan with a cruciform arrangement of rather elaborate double-border elements. There are actually three different designs in all, with one repeat.

A

B

C

Ancient Pueblo pottery. A: Bird design from Homolobi on a food bowl, apparently a unique example of decoration. B: Bird figure on a bowl from Chaves Pass. Toothed birds are often found in ancient Pueblo pictography. C: Design on the interior of a bowl, with four parts of a double border cut up and fitted into a concave surface; from the area of Tusayan.

Ancient Pueblo pottery. A: Spiral design on a food bowl from Four-Mile Ruin, Arizona. The spiral is one of the most characteristic designs found on pottery from the Little Colorado ruins. B: Vase from Chevlon Ruin, Arizona, with geometric decoration of meanders, zigzags and bands.

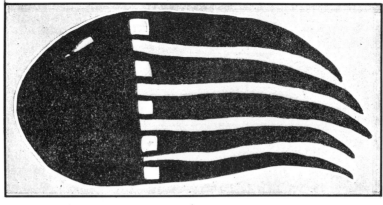

A

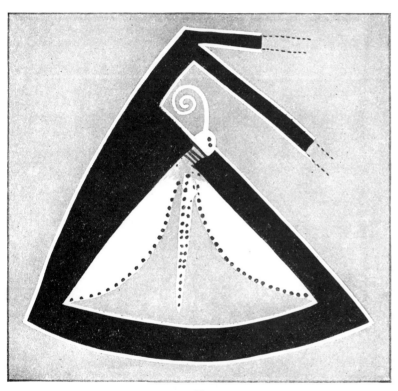

B

C

D

Ancient Pueblo pottery. A: Bear-paw design found on the exterior of a food bowl from Four-Mile Ruin. B: "Butterfly" design found on a food bowl from Four-Mile Ruin. C: Bird design on a food bowl from the ruins of old Shumopovi. The head resembles the mask of a katcina personated in Tusayan pueblo. D: Geometrical design from a food bowl from Four-Mile Ruin consisting of triangles, T-figures and terraced designs.

Ancient Pueblo pottery. A, B: Bird designs on food bowls from Shumopovi, one somewhat conventionalized, the other entirely symbolic. C: Twin-bird design on the exterior of a food bowl from Pinedale, Arizona. D: Mythic bird and game of chance from a design on a food bowl from Shumopovi. E: Bird design from the exterior of a food bowl from Four-Mile Ruin. The bird figure is remarkable for the distinctive rendering of the feet and tail.

Ancient Pueblo pottery. Segments of border designs from interiors of food bowls, analyzed and redrawn on straight, flat surfaces.

Ancient Pueblo pottery designs and borders. A: Spirals. B: Stepped frets. C: Meanders and dots. D: Border of interlaced frets. E: Spirals, cross or star, and diagonal bands of triangles. F: Stepped frets.

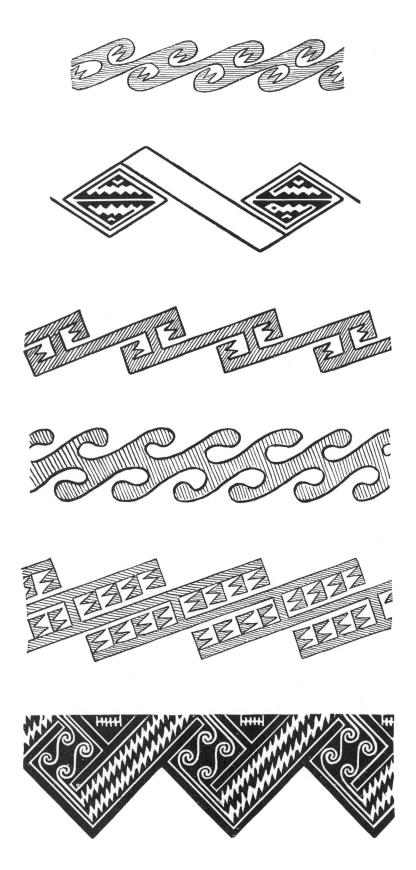

Ancient Pueblo pottery. Border designs, either simple single elements, or complex designs built up of simple elements, such as meanders, zigzags and spiral shapes.

A

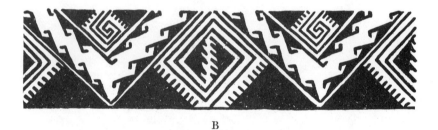

B

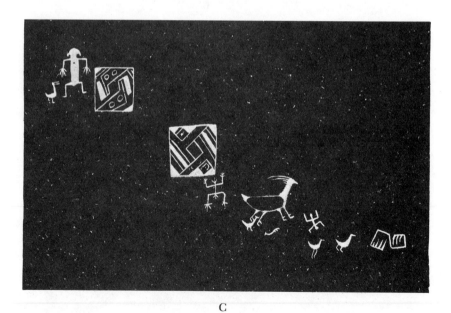

C

Pueblo pottery. A: Vase with triangle-pattern decoration. B: Flat drawing of a triangle pattern found on an earthenware bowl. Triangular patterns were not common in the ancient Pueblo pottery of Arizona, New Mexico and Colorado, and the motif may have come from southern Arizona. It is identified as representing the head feathers of the quail. C: Pictographs on the walls of the Cañon de Chelly, with conventionalized figures of men, birds and deer, and various geometrical designs. The pictographs were found in connection with a small storage cist (roofed pit).

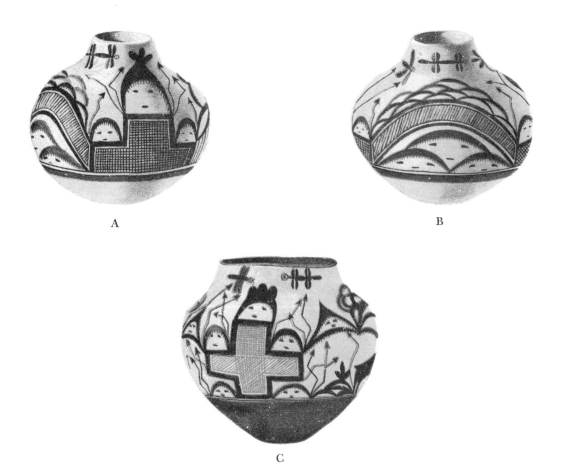

A   B

C

D

Pueblo pottery. Ceremonial water vases made by the Sia (Tsia). D shows the unit of design on C drawn out as a continuous flat border. Sia potters were noted for their use of realistic animal motifs and the "cross" or "star."

Pueblo pottery. A: Zuñi water vase with a combination of conventionalized and naturalistic designs. B: Laguna water vase with a seminaturalistic design. C: Zuñi water-vase design made up of simple geometric components. D: Zuñi water vase with leaves and meanders used in stripes. E: Zuñi water vase. F: Laguna water vase with a naturalistic bird and conventionalized designs. As would be expected, water vessels are the most common form of pottery made in an arid climate.

Pueblo pottery. A, B, F: Zuñi water vases with various geometric, naturalistic and curvilinear designs. C: Laguna water vase with scroll and wave design. D: Water vase from the Cañon de Chelly with stripes and Greek fret applied in a vertical swirl. E: Acoma pot with a combination of naturalistic and conventionalized designs.

Pueblo pottery. A, C–G: Laguna pottery showing typical decoration, including a wide use of naturalistic designs. Birds were a frequent motif on Laguna pottery decoration. B: Water vessel from the Cañon de Chelly with diamond motifs. H, I: Acoma pottery, with a style of decoration combining naturalistic and geometric designs.

Pueblo pottery. A: Water vessel from the Cañon de Chelly with decorations composed of stepped triangles, frets, circles and meanders. B, C, E–G: Laguna bowls and water vases with typical combinations of geometric and naturalistic designs. D: Zuñi water vase with naturalistic and geometric designs.

Pueblo pottery. Laguna effigies in white decorated ware in the form of birds, quadrupeds and mythical animals; such effigies were usually hollowed out to serve as drinking vessels. The animals include (A) sheep, (B) antelope, (C) dog or coyote.

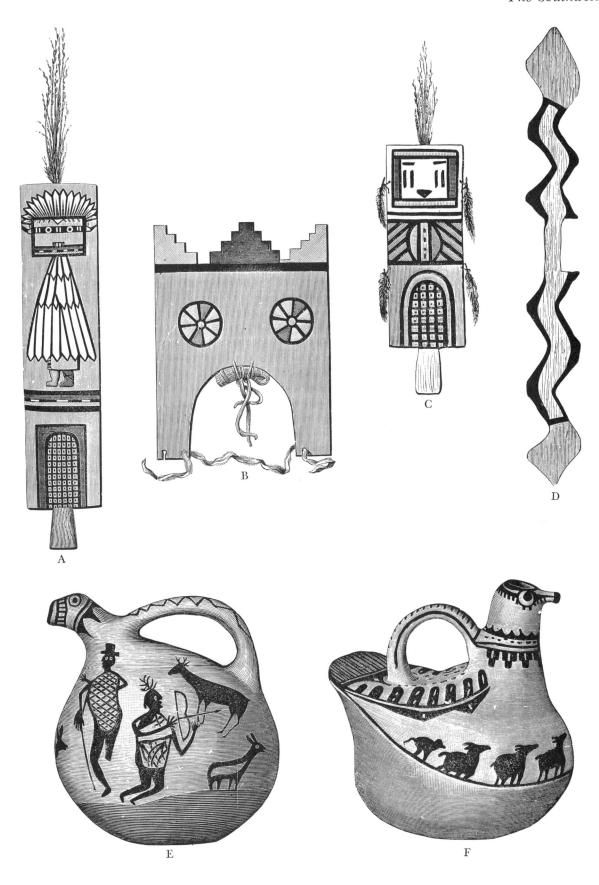

Pueblo art. A–D: Walpi dance ornaments. A and C are painted sticks carried in the hand, B is a headdress, D is a stick painted to represent lightning. E, F: Cochiti white-ware pottery decorated in black with unusual designs. E is a hunting scene, F shows goats herded by a dog, painted on a bird-shaped body.

Zuñi masks. Front and back views of the mask of Hemishikwe, worn in the autumn festival. Masks worn by personators of such figures are all alike except for tablet and decoration.

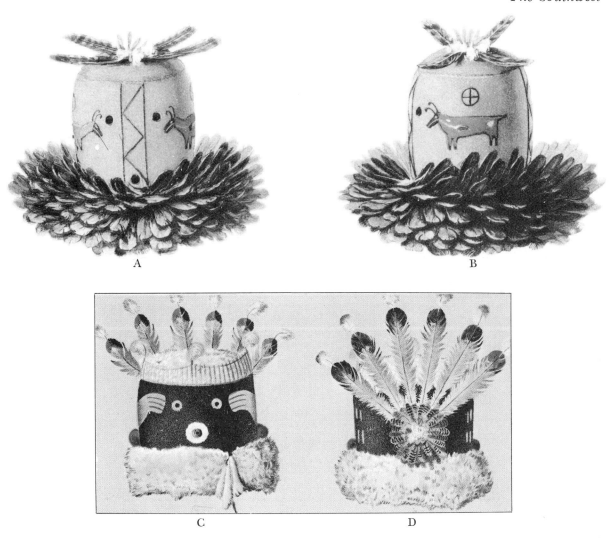

A, B: Front and side views of the Zuñi mask of Nawisho, one of the most attractive masks in the autumn festival. C–F: Sia masks representing the Kasuma, supernatural beings who accompanied the Sia on their journey to this world. Dances featuring these masks were usually held to summon rain or snow.

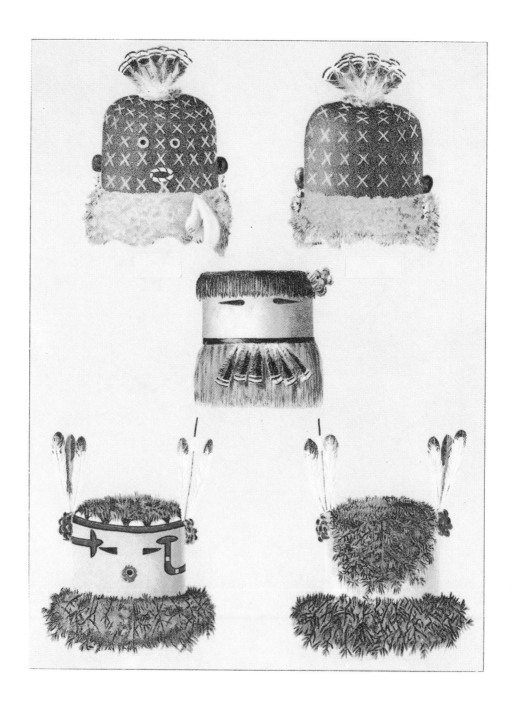

Masks of the Sia, also worn by personators of the Kasuma in Sia dances. The Sia, though greatly reduced in numbers, maintained an active ceremonial life into the twentieth century, and possessed a great variety of masks, some very old.

Zuñi masks of gods and goddesses accompanying the Hemishikwe in the dances of the great autumn festival. Masks were only part of the elaborate costumes worn by dancers in these festivals.

Zuñi masks. A–C: Side, back and front views of one of the styles of Hehea masks, used in the ceremonies of the council of the gods. This mask represents Hehea, "The Blunderer," of the Nadir, one of the six directions acknowledged by the Zuñi. The lines from his eyes represent rain, not tears. E, F: Front and back views of the mask of Uwannami, the Rainmaker, with symbols of lightning and clouds and bear tracks (on the cheeks) representing the marks an animal makes on soft, well-watered earth.

Zuñi masks. A, B: Side and front views of Pautiwa, a member of the council of the gods who appeared three times annually in Zuñi pueblo. This ceremony took place at the winter solstice. C, D: Front and side views of Kwelele, the Firemaker, also used in the winter-solstice festival.

Zuñi masks. More masks of the Muluktatkia, gods who appeared in the autumn festival.
A: Natashku. B–D: Front, side and back views of another mask. These figures also wore
elaborate costumes.

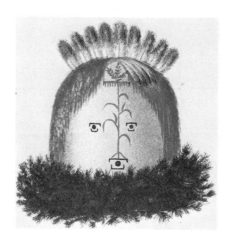

Navaho ceremonial masks, many made in the Zuñi style. They were used in ceremonies by personators of gods; sometimes they were placed on invalids in healing ceremonies. Such masks had to be made from the skins of deer that were smothered, not shot. If they were made from the hide of an animal shot by a bullet, according to Navaho belief, the wearer would die of fever.

Zuñi masks. Masks of warriors of the Zenith and of the Nadir (two of the six directions acknowledged by the Zuñi, and sometimes referred to as the heavens and the underworld). These warrior masks refer to a tribe once inimical to the Zuñi, but later adopted into the Zuñi tribe. The dance at which these masks were used was held once every four years.

Zuñi masks. A: Yamuhakto, the attendant of the priest Hututu. B C,: Front and side views of the mask of the Salamobiya (warrior) of the Nadir, with a collar of raven plumes. This mask was worn in the autumn festival.

Zuñi masks. A: Front view of the mask of the priest Hututu. B, C: Front and side views of the mask of the Salamobiya (warrior) of the Zenith, with a collar of raven feathers. The body of the dancer wearing this mask was painted to match the design on the mask. D: Side view of the mask of the Rain Priest of the North, worn at the council of the gods and at the great autumn festival. The front view is on the facing page.

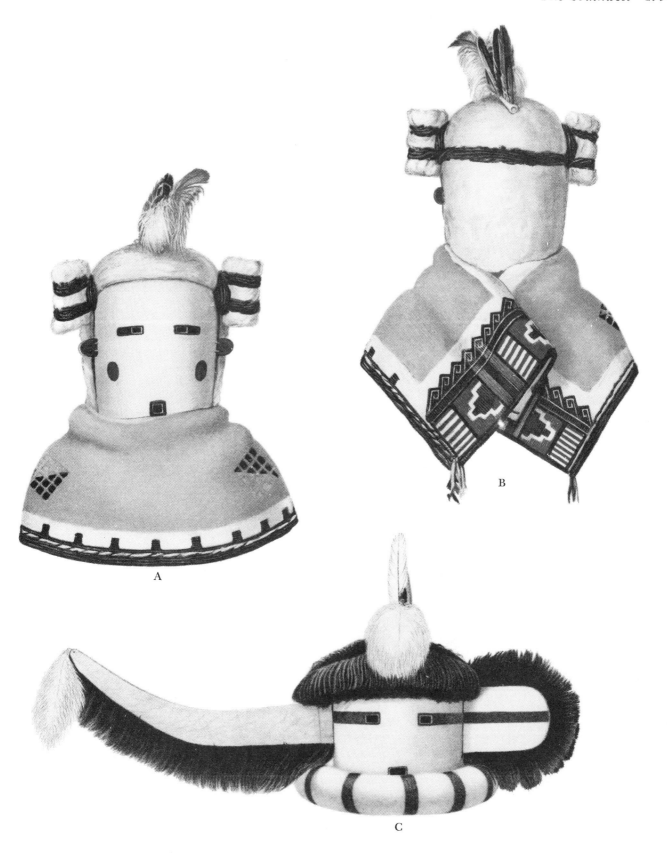

Zuñi masks. A, B: Front and back views of the mask of Komokattsi. C: Front view of mask D on the facing page.

Zuñi masks. A: Koyemshi, one of the "old dance men," one of whom is said to have invented masks. These masks were worn in a burlesquing dance. B, C: Back and front views of Tkianilona, "Owner of the Springs," greatest of the Zuñi ancestral gods.

Zuñi masks. Group of masks worn by the Salamobiya (warriors), representing the six directions of the Zuñi: North (A), East (B), West (C), South (D), Heavens, or Zenith (E), and Earth, or Underworld, or Nadir (F).

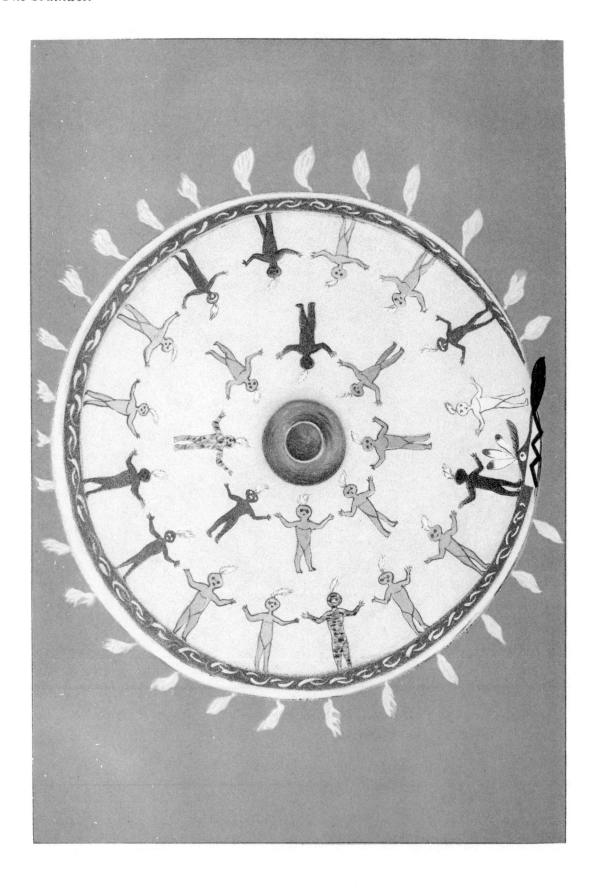

Zuñi sand painting used as an altar in the Kiva of the North at Zuñi pueblo, during an initiation ceremony held only every four years. The figures represent the Salamobiya, and were painted in colors and patterns representing those warriors of the six directions. The group of figures is surrounded by a plumed serpent.

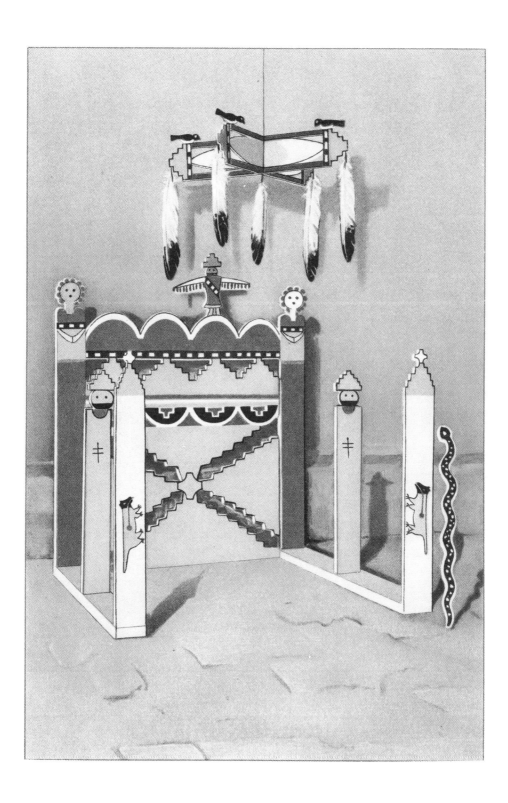

Zuñi altar erected for nighttime ceremonies by the Tsaniakiakwe or Hunter Fraternity.
These ceremonies were held during the great autumnal festival. The altar is shown before
the beginning of a sacred meal-painting on the floor.

Sia altar and sand painting for rain ceremonials of the Knife Society. The painting was done with black pigment and powdered kaolin.

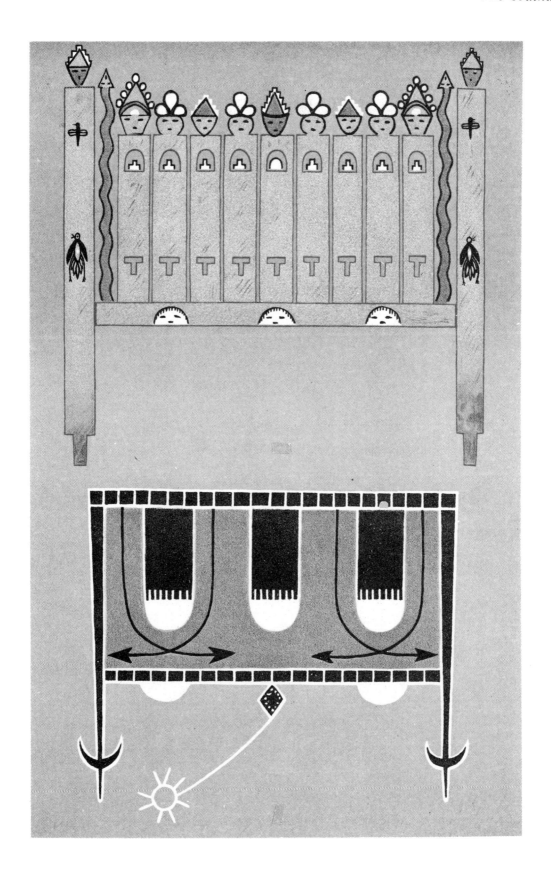

Sia slat altar and sand painting prepared for the rain ceremonial of the Giant Society.

Sia altar and sand painting of the Snake Society, a very important organization in Sia life. Aspirants to this society had to spend two years undergoing various degrees of initiation before they became full members.

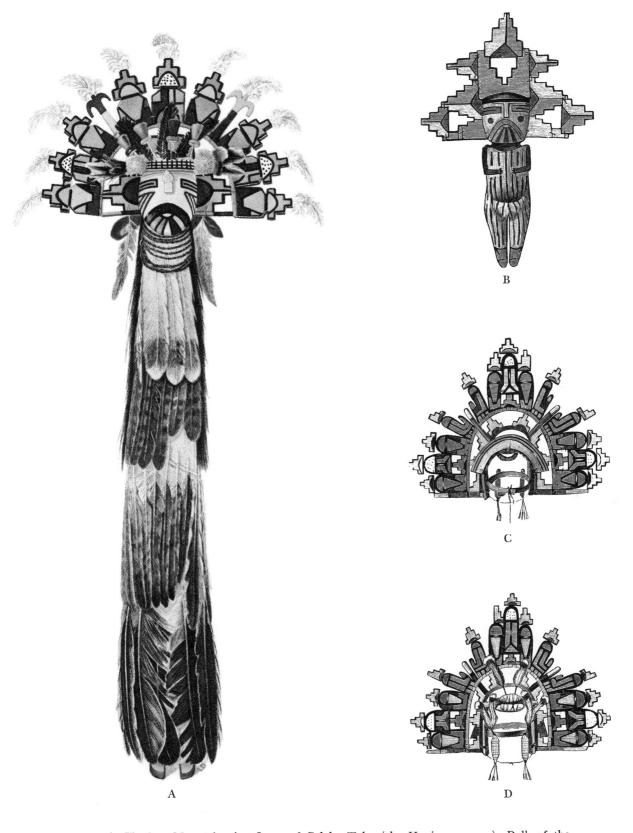

A: Hopi or Moqui katcina figure of Calako Taka (the Hopi corn man). Dolls of the katcina figures were used to teach children to recognize the symbolism of the various katcinas when they appeared in the dances, but were not considered themselves sacred. However, large figures of Calako Taka or Calako Mana (Corn Maiden) were sometimes introduced into ceremonies, and manipulated as puppets in the dances. B: Doll, showing the mode of wearing a maskette headdress. C, D: Front and rear views of a Hopi headdress, recalling some of the Aztec headdresses.

Zuñi fetish and shield, used by members of the highly secret Zuñi society known as the Priesthood of the Bow.

Fetish and shield of the Zuñi Priesthood of the Bow.

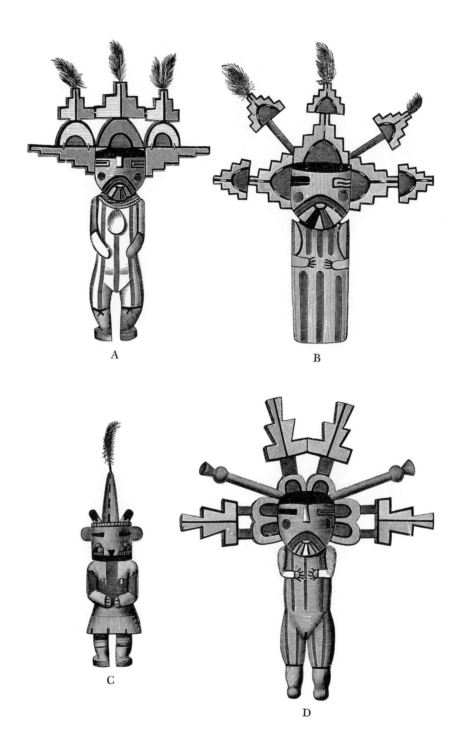

Hopi effigies from Walpi pueblo. The figures are made of wood, and the decorations painted on, although A has a necklace added and C has a cloth skirt attached as well. A, B and C also have feathers attached.

Shinumo statuettes, objects of worship in one form or another. Made of wood, they were painted and had various feathers or other decorations attached.

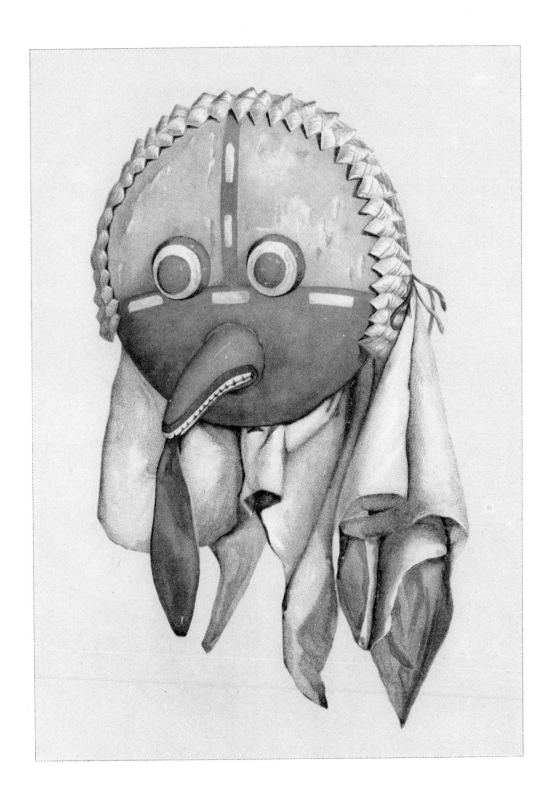

Powamu mask used in the Hopi nine-day ceremonials, one of the most elaborate rites in which katcinas appeared. Between uses, the katcina masks were guarded carefully by their owners or wearers, and were frequently spoken to, being addressed as "my friend" or "my double."

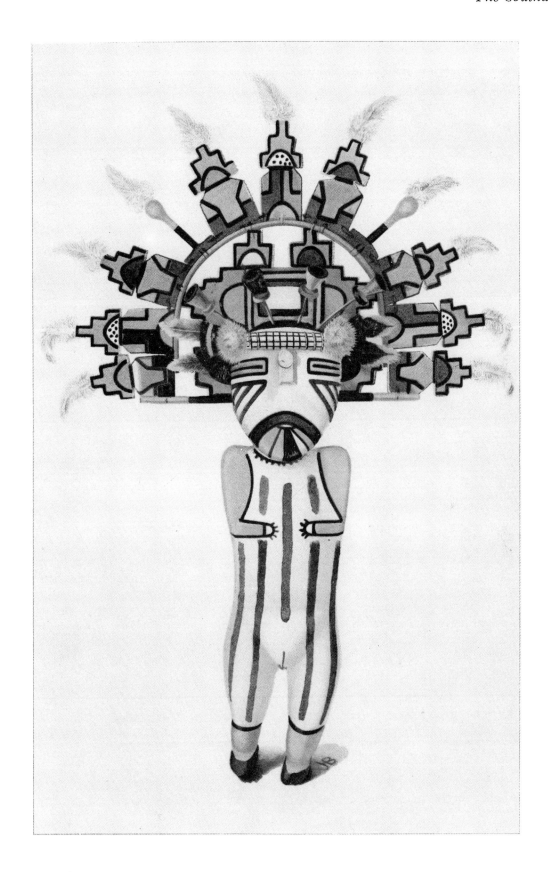

Hopi katcina, a doll of the Calako Mana (Corn Maiden), a female deity wearing a stepped headdress. This doll represents a katcina that appeared in the Palulukonti rites in Tusayan in 1893.

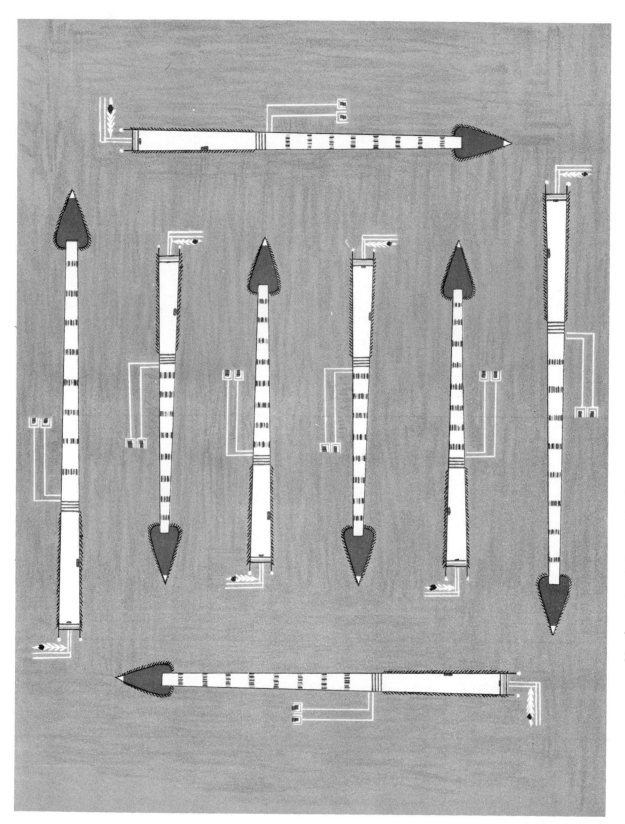

Navaho sand painting used in the ceremonial of the Mountain Chant. Five colors of sand were used in making the painting: black from powdered charcoal; white from white sandstone; yellow from yellow sandstone; blue (gray) from a mixture of black and white for large areas; powdered turquoise, malachite or indigo for small areas.

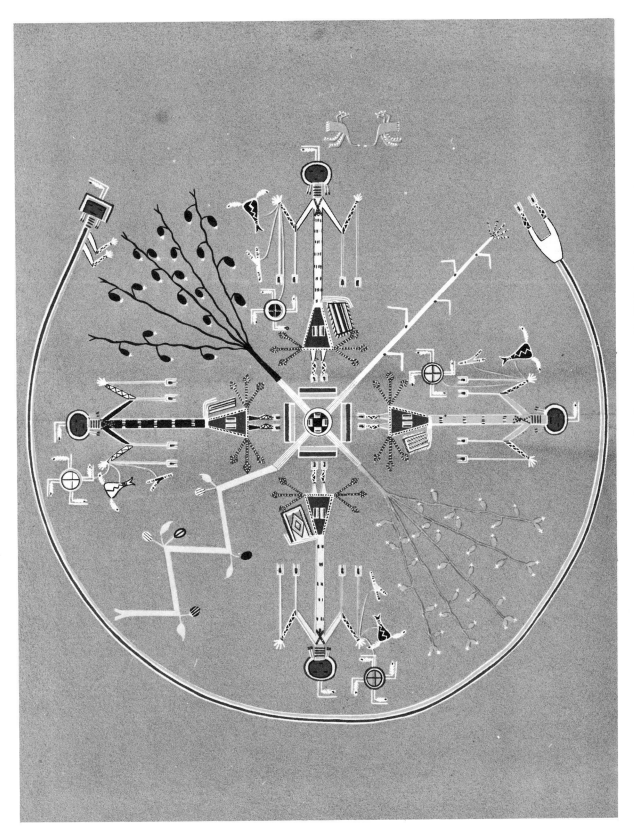

Navaho sand painting from the Mountain Chant ceremonial. This painting represents something the prophet saw in the home of the Bears in the legend on which the ceremonial is based. The four figures represent four gods surrounded by the rainbow deity.

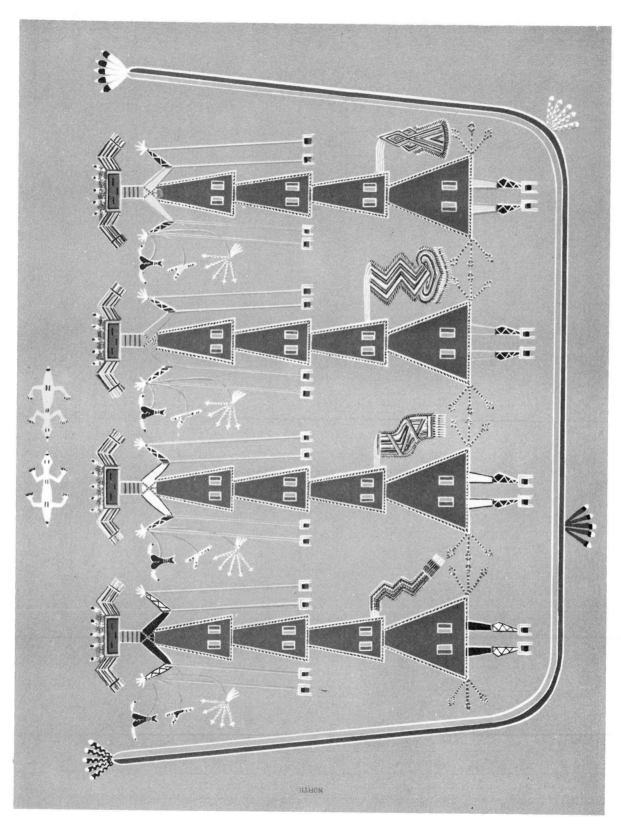

NORTH

Navaho sand painting from the Mountain Chant ceremonial. This scene commemorates a visit to the Lodge of Dew in the Mountain Chant legend. Each figure (all are goddesses with rectangular heads) is shown clad in four garments because no single garment could clothe so gigantic a personage.

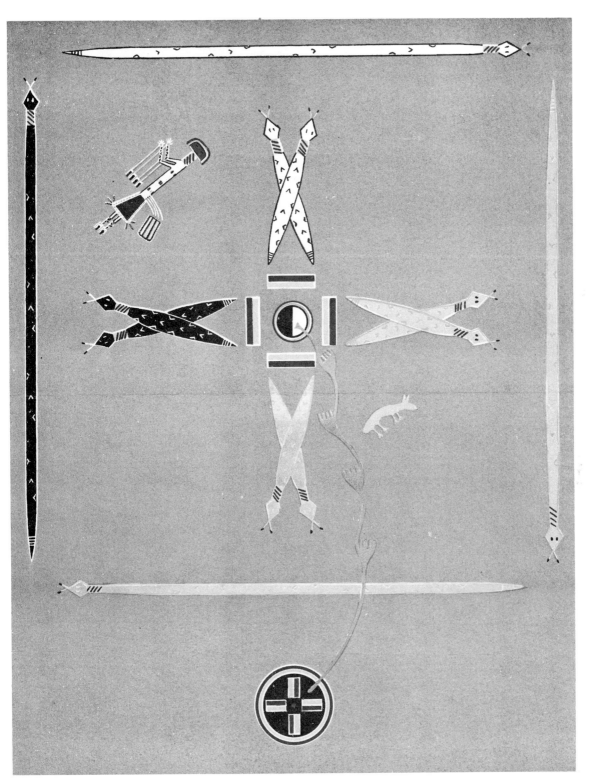

Navaho sand painting from the Mountain Chant ceremonial. Each painting was erased at the end of the day's ceremonial, and a new one commenced on the successive day. Each painting had to be done between dawn and sunset, so that large elaborate paintings required several artists working simultaneously while one man continuously ground colors to keep them supplied. Though the Mountain Chant was primarily a healing ritual, sometimes initiation of children of the tribe would take place in the same ceremony.

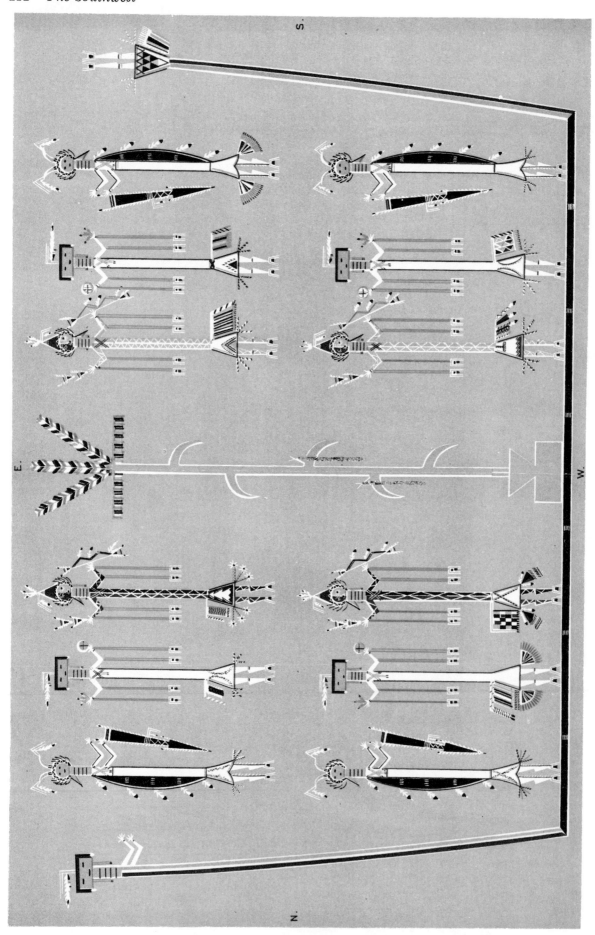

Navaho sand painting from the Mountain Chant ceremonial. This particular ceremony was held at Fort Wingate, Arizona, in the early 1890s. The painting was done in quarters, each artist attempting to finish his segment first. During the work, wagers were made among the spectators on which painter would be the winner. The cornstalk at the center of the design represents the substance of life.

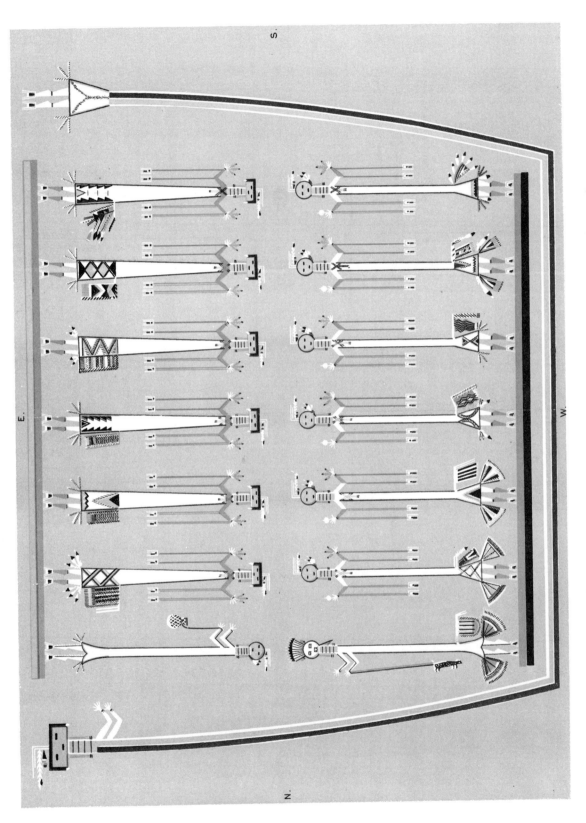

Navaho sand painting from the Mountain Chant ceremonies held at Fort Wingate. Several artists worked on this painting from dawn till after three o'clock on a December afternoon, while a paint grinder was kept busy supplying them with colors. The figures with round heads are male deities and those with rectangular heads female deities. The necessity for employing a large number of painters for the Mountain Chant sand paintings was one of the reasons for the great expense of holding the ceremony, and the rarity of its occurrence.

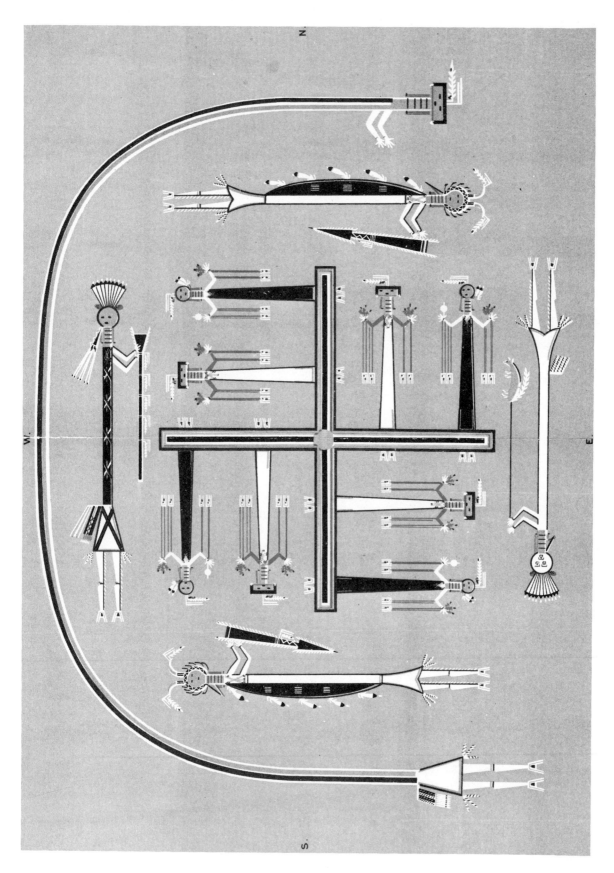

Navaho sand painting from the Mountain Chant ceremonial. This was made by four artists, each working on an arm of the central cross, and then working from the center of the design out. The work began at daylight and lasted until late afternoon. During the ceremonies of the night following the completion of this painting, the invalid for whose benefit the ceremony was held sat in the center of the painting.

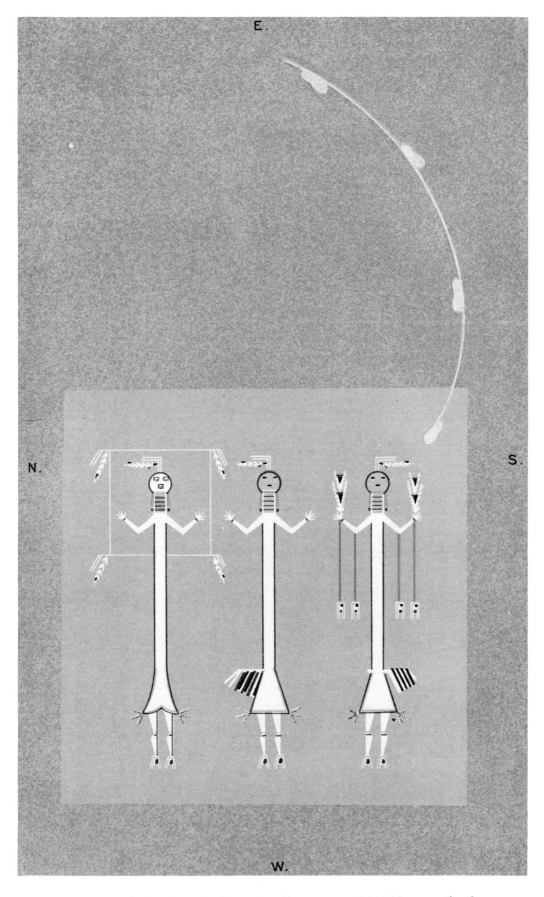

Navaho sand painting from the Mountain Chant ceremonial. This was painted on a square of sand three inches deep, much as an artist might paint on a canvas. Here, too, the artists worked from early morning till sundown. After the proper rituals had been held, the picture was erased in preparation for the next work.

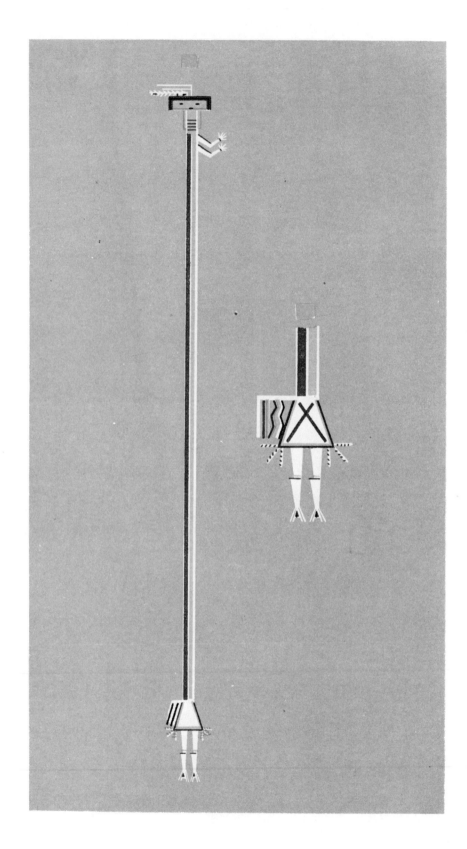

Navaho sand painting covering one of four sweat houses specially built in conjunction with the performance of the Mountain Chant ceremony. The eastern and western houses had this figure of a rainbow bent over the entire huts, painted by three young men under the direction of priests.

Ancient Pueblo art. Basketwork shield from a cliff dwelling, featuring a naturalistic figure derived from a frog.

Navaho blankets. A: Blanket of old-style design, made of native yarn in natural colors of white, black, dark blue, pale blue and bayeta red. B: Tufted rug, somewhat like an Oriental carpet in effect, made of shredded red flannel (bayeta) with designs in yellow, dark blue and green. C: Blanket of finest quality made by a man many considered to be the best weaver in his tribe. The yarn used was commercial Germantown yarn. Elaborate designs like those on this blanket were sometimes drawn first on the sand by the weaver; otherwise, the artists worked only from designs in their heads.

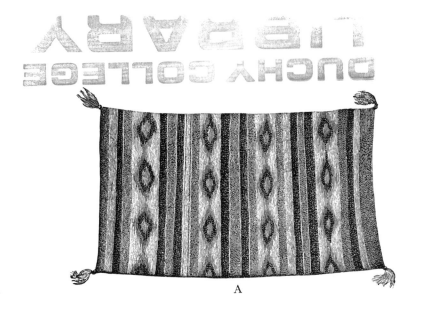

A

B

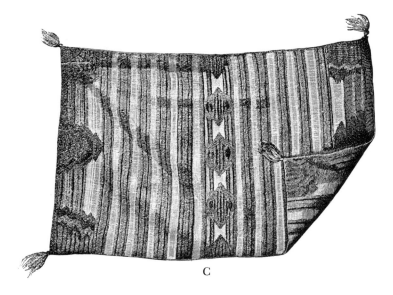

C

Navaho blankets. A: Small blanket with design in gaudy colors made of native yarns. This type of blanket was commonly worn by a woman. B, C: Two small half-size blankets made either for children's wear or for use as saddle blankets. The regular design of the border of blanket B is quite rare in Navaho weaving.